The Modern Language Association of America

Approaches to Teaching
Masterpieces of World Literature

Joseph Gibaldi, Series Editor

1. Joseph Gibaldi, ed. *Approaches to Teaching Chaucer's* Canterbury Tales. 1980.
2. Carole Slade, ed. *Approaches to Teaching Dante's* Divine Comedy. 1982.
3. Richard Bjornson, ed. *Approaches to Teaching Cervantes'* Don Quixote. 1984.
4. Jess B. Bessinger, Jr., and Robert F. Yeager, eds. *Approaches to Teaching* Beowulf. 1984.
5. Richard J. Dunn, ed. *Approaches to Teaching Dickens'* David Copperfield. 1984.

Approaches to Teaching Dickens'
David Copperfield

Edited by

Richard J. Dunn

The Modern Language Association of America
New York   1984

Copyright © 1984 by The Modern Language Association of America

Library of Congress Cataloging in Publication Data

Main entry under title:

Approaches to teaching Dickens' David Copperfield.

(Approaches to teaching masterpieces of world
literature ; 5)
    Bibliography: p.
    Includes index.
    1. Dickens, Charles, 1812–1870. David Copperfield—
Addresses, essays, lectures.   2. Dickens, Charles, 1812–
1870—Study and teaching—Addresses, essays, lectures.
I. Dunn, Richard J., 1938–   . II. Series.
PR4558.A76   1984   823′.8   84-1046
ISBN 0-87352-483-7
ISBN 0-87352-484-5 (pbk.)

Cover illustration in the paperback edition: Hablot
K. Browne, illustration for *David Copperfield*,
chapter 17.

Published by The Modern Language Association of America
62 Fifth Avenue, New York, New York 10011

CONTENTS

PREFACE TO THE SERIES

In his thoughtful and sensitive book *The Art of Teaching*, Gilbert Highet wrote, "Bad teaching wastes a great deal of effort, and spoils many lives which might have been full of energy and happiness." All too many teachers have failed in their work, Highet argued, simply "because they have not thought about it." We hope that the Approaches to Teaching Masterpieces of World Literature series, sponsored by the Modern Language Association's Committee on Teaching and Related Professional Activities, will not only improve the craft—as well as the art—of teaching but also encourage serious and continuing discussion of the aims and methods of our teaching.

The principal objective of the series is to collect within each volume a number of points of view on teaching a particular work of world literature that is widely taught at the undergraduate level. The preparation of each volume begins with a survey of instructors who have considerable experience in teaching the work. The survey enables us to include in the volume the philosophies and approaches, thoughts and methods of scores of experienced teachers. The result is a sourcebook of material, information, and ideas on teaching the work to undergraduates.

The series is intended to serve nonspecialists as well as specialists, inexperienced as well as experienced teachers, graduate students who wish to learn effective ways of teaching as well as senior professors who wish to compare their own approaches with the approaches of colleagues in other schools. Of course, no volume in the series can ever substitute for erudition, intelligence, creativity, and sensitivity in teaching. We hope merely that each book will point readers in useful directions; at most each will offer only a first step in the long journey to successful teaching.

In a time that increasingly demands a rededication to undergraduate teaching of the humanities and to the idea of a liberal education, it may well be that our sometimes divided and fragmented profession will rediscover in its concern for and commitment to teaching a sense of purpose, unity, and community that many believe it presently lacks. We hope that the Approaches to Teaching Masterpieces of World Literature series will serve in some small way to refocus attention on the importance of teaching and to improve undergraduate instruction. We may perhaps adopt as keynote for the series Alfred North Whitehead's observation in *The Aims of Education* that a liberal education "proceeds by imparting a knowledge of the masterpieces of thought, of imaginative literature, and of art."

Joseph Gibaldi
Series Editor

PREFACE TO THE VOLUME

Including a volume on Charles Dickens in a series on teaching masterpieces of world literature seems appropriate, but the reasons for basing this volume on *David Copperfield* may be less apparent. Dickensians generally disagree over their nominations for the best Dickens novel—for some it is *Great Expectations*; for others, *Bleak House, Our Mutual Friend,* or even *Pickwick Papers.* But *David Copperfield*, since first appearing serially in 1849–50, has remained a popular classic, and in the past thirty years its biographical, social, and psychological elements have attracted increasing academic interest. Therefore, in today's college and university courses *David Copperfield* serves not only to introduce Dickens or the novel but also to demonstrate the relations of fiction and autobiography, the roles of myth, archetype, and fantasy in fiction. Essays in this volume describe the many ways teachers use *David Copperfield* in courses of varied subject emphasis, size, and student experience. Like other volumes in the series, the present book concerns teaching at the undergraduate level, and the intention throughout is to assist the nonspecialist as well as the teacher more experienced in Dickens, the novel, and Victorian literature.

There are two parts to the book: Materials and Approaches. The selective and evaluative Materials section discusses the relative merits of available paperback editions, recommends background and required student readings, and lists some aids to teaching. Recommendations for the instructor's library include a selection of the many reference works, textual studies, biographical and critical commentaries. Much information in this first part comes from more than one hundred responses to the survey of Dickens teachers that preceded preparation of this volume.

In the second part, Approaches, sixteen teachers discuss their classroom use of *David Copperfield.* Many of the instructors explain critical and historical assumptions underlying their choice of the work, and the teaching strategies frequently illustrate critical stances these teachers strive to develop in their students, but the essays remain pedagogical discussions, designed to describe the teaching of *David Copperfield.* Some of the teachers have arrived at their present methods after considerable trial and error, but none advocates a single method or narrow objective in teaching *David Copperfield.* The introduction to part 2 more specifically surveys the range of the sixteen essays, all of which confirm my sense that dynamic fiction requires dynamic teaching. As J. Gill Holland writes, "One of the chief delights of reading Dickens is to let the imagination go." So, too, may teaching Dickens become a rewarding imaginative activity.

My primary acknowledgment is to Joseph Gibaldi, general editor of this series. He has provided sound advice at all stages of the work, from initial proposal and survey of instructors through final drafts. I am grateful, too, for the patient professionalism of the essay authors, who all responded graciously to the special demands of writing about teaching. Working independently, they frequently complemented one another; appearing together, they form a symposium that should gather in person to discuss issues readers of their essays will surely identify. I am grateful to George H. Ford, Coral Lansbury, James Kincaid, and Garrett Stewart for consultation at different stages of the project. Although they have not written essays for the volume, their Dickens scholarship has greatly influenced me and other teachers of *David Copperfield*, and I value the advice they have provided as consultants for this book.

RJD

Part One

MATERIALS

Richard J. Dunn

Editions

Teachers of *Bleak House* or *Hard Times* have a clear-cut choice between an authoritative text in a critical edition and a number of other less satisfactory paperback editions, but no single edition of *David Copperfield* was preferred by participants in the survey of Dickens teachers. In 1983 six paperback editions were available: Airmont, Bantam Classic, Penguin, Riverside, Signet, and World's Classics. Ninety-five percent of the survey respondents use three of these texts: Penguin (40%), Riverside (40%), Signet (15%). Many instructors pointed out needs that no present text meets, and all reported advantages and disadvantages of the editions they use. The following discussion describes the features of the available texts and includes teachers' opinions about the quality of text, introductions, notes, and physical format.

The Penguin *David Copperfield*, edited by Trevor Blount, satisfies many classroom requirements. It has a reliable text and includes a number of the original illustrations. Blount provides a helpful introduction, footnotes, and brief biographical sketch of Dickens, and he identifies monthly number divisions in the text (asterisks preceding the chapters that began the original monthly parts) and in the table of contents. This edition reprints Dickens' preface from the first edition (1850) and also the revised preface he wrote in 1867 for the *Copperfield* volume of the Charles Dickens Edition, the last published in his lifetime. Collating the 1850 and 1867 editions, Blount has produced a clean text, regularizing a number of Dickens' peculiar spellings and silently correcting obvious misprints. For rhetorical effect, he retains the punctuation of the 1850 version, which reinforces the sense that many of Dickens' original readers read the book aloud. The Penguin does not include passages Dickens cut from proofs when his monthly numbers overran page limitations.

Many instructors choose the Penguin because it is the only paperback edition to offer a good selection of the illustrations (twenty-three of the original thirty-eight). Each monthly part contained two drawings by Dickens' frequent illustrator, Hablot K. Browne, known as "Phiz." Often containing the inspiration for stage and film adaptations and capturing the flavor of Dickensian scene and character, the illustrations are useful to teachers. The Penguin *Copperfield* also includes facsimiles of the monthly cover design and the illustrated title page to the first bound edition. Several teachers criticized not only the absence of the remaining illustrations but also the quality of reproduction—compared with those of the Oxford Illustrated Dickens and the recent Clarendon *David Copperfield*, which as hardbound volumes use higher-quality paper, the Penguin illlustrations are of relatively poor quality.

Blount's introduction is helpful both for first readers and those generally familiar with the novel. He locates *David Copperfield* in the history of the novel, noting Dickens' indebtedness to the great eighteenth-century novelists and acknowledging Dickens' influence on Tolstoy, Dostoevsky, and Joyce; points out but does not overstress the autobiographical qualities of *David Copperfield* as he argues that "Dickens goes far beyond the explicit novelist qualities that he bestows on David" (15); describes some effects of serial publication on this novel; and mentions its documentary interest in several topics of the late 1840s. Seven pages of explanatory footnotes assist modern readers with many topical and literary references, but, as teachers pointed out, a more extensive annotation would be helpful for American students.

Instructors who use the Penguin edition do so because it provides a satisfactory text, illustrations, and Blount's valuable introduction and notes—all at a reasonable price. Those who object to it consider the print too small and the margins too narrow for students' notations. A few complain that the print may smear and the binding not hold up well, and some regret that it includes neither the passages Dickens cut from the proofs nor the working notes he prepared as number plans while writing the novel. (Only the recent World's Classics edition provides the number plans, but this edition, unlike the Bantam, Riverside, and Signet, does not include the proof deletions.)

The Riverside *Copperfield*, edited by George H. Ford, is as popular as the Penguin among the instructors surveyed. Many teachers consider the Riverside (currently a dollar and a half more expensive than the Penguin) a better buy because they find its binding more durable and its text more attractive. The print is large and clear, and the margins are generous, especially at the binding. Ford provides a fine introduction, textual and bibliographical note, and sketch of Dickens' early life, and he includes facsimiles of the monthly parts' covers and of Dickens' preface to the Charles Dickens Edition. The major passages omitted from the proof sheets of *David Copperfield* appear for the first time with an edition of the novel; because Dickens never restored them to the novel, Ford thinks it appropriate to keep them apart from the text in an appendix.

A number of teachers commented on the high quality of Ford's critical introduction to the Riverside edition. Ford discusses the book's popular and classic status and notes that children and adults read it differently. He finds that much humor remains for adult readers, but that for them it often seems a sadder book. Ford also describes Dickens' complex treatment of childhood and the way he transformed fact into fiction. With concise comments on Dickens' handling of detail and on his dramatic structuring of episodes, Ford anticipates many concerns of later critics.

Although this edition contains no illustrations and no explanatory footnotes, teachers praise its quality. One of the first reliable paperback editions of a Dickens novel, the Riverside *Copperfield* has the advantage of nearly twenty-five years of use. As one instructor remarks, "certain texts appear in courses by habit."

The Signet *David Copperfield*, with an afterword by Edgar Johnson, was the first edition to restore Dickens' proof deletions to the text, identifying them by brackets. Asterisks between new monthly chapters help readers recognize the original part divisions. The preface to the Charles Dickens Edition is included, but there are no illustrations and no notes. In his afterword, Johnson, the author of the standard modern Dickens biography, deals mainly with the novel as a work of literary art and only slightly with its relation to Dickens' life. Johnson provides a selected bibliography of Dickens' other writing and of biography and criticism.

Several of the survey respondents expressed concern over the apparent size of the modern editions, for they do not want to discourage students by presenting them with a long work that seems even longer in paperback format. Several teachers favor the Riverside edition because it accommodates *David Copperfield* and supplementary material in 678 large pages. Others, however, follow the same rationale in opting for the 880-page Signet, which has a tight binding, smaller print, and narrow margins and thus seems considerably shorter than the Penguin edition.

Teachers who use the Airmont and Bantam editions indicated price as their principal criterion. The Airmont provides a brief introduction by Mary M. Threapleton, who, despite her attention to the book's autobiographical quality, regards David as the novel's least interesting character. Hers is the least thorough of the available introductions, and no instructor indicated that her comments were useful. The Airmont contains the preface to the Charles Dickens Edition but no illustrations, notes, or indications of number divisions; it has crowded and poor-quality type.

The Bantam edition appeared in 1981, too recently for many of the surveyed instructors to have become familiar with it. Except for a single-page sketch of Dickens' career (without even mentioning *David Copperfield*), it contains no editorial apparatus or commentary, but it does have the prefaces to the first edition and the Charles Dickens Edition. It incorporates the deletions Dickens made from proofs but—unlike the Signet and Riverside texts—does not identify them.

Edited by Nina Burgis and based on her definitive 1981 hardbound Clarendon edition, the World's Classics paperback offers several advantages: It has the most accurate text available (therefore omitting those passages Dickens never restored from proof) and contains a lucid introduction, numerous explanatory notes, and both the original and the 1867 prefaces. Reproduction of the trial titles Dickens tested and of his monthly number plans is a unique feature of this text. Regrettably, Burgis includes only eight of the original illustrations. The explanatory footnotes should be useful to American instructors, because they explain literary allusions, geographical sites, and unusual language features. The sole reminders of the superb textual apparatus in the parent Clarendon edition are a few notes that show differences between manuscript or proof and text. Generally a sound edition, the World's Classics paperback has small but clear print.

When ordering a *David Copperfield* text, an instructor must anticipate whether students will benefit from editorial assistance—especially from restoration of the deleted passages—and also whether study of the novel will include some attention to the illustrations. Many instructors would prefer an edition similar to the Norton critical editions of *Hard Times* and *Bleak House*. Ideally, they would like an edition containing the surviving bit of autobiography that was Dickens' germ for the novel, a complete set of the illustrations, and more annotation for students.

Required and Recommended Student Reading

Because in most courses the reading of *David Copperfield* requires two weeks and because the courses usually include other long novels, instructors tend not to assign great amounts of secondary reading. A few actively discourage it, and one even says he would forbid students to read background studies "if that prohibition were not likely to increase their dependence on such materials." Respondents to the survey mentioned more than fifty books and essays that they recommend to students, and many of these recommendations reflect the special interests of courses and instructors. The following lists include those works most frequently mentioned as useful for acquainting students with the Victorian period, Dickens in general, the autobiographical elements of *David Copperfield*, critical and textual issues, and other Dickens works. For more extensive discussion of these materials, see The Instructor's Library.

Background on the Victorian Period

A number of instructors highly recommended Walter Houghton's *The Victorian Frame of Mind* as a comprehensive survey of ideas and attitudes. Its sections on love, earnestness, and enthusiasm are particularly useful in providing a context for considering David as a character of his time and for discussing the relation of David to the various women in his story. Richard D. Altick's *Victorian People and Ideas* provides background information about religious movements, the status of women, and the place of art in society. Henry Mayhew's *London Labour and the London Poor*, a collection of newspaper articles begun in 1849, provides an encyclopedic and well-illustrated view of mid-nineteenth-century urban society.

Introductions to Dickens

To supplement introductory material in the texts, instructors frequently recommend several works that survey Dickens' career or point out particular qualities of his writing. The most frequently recommended general introductions are E. D. H. Johnson's *Charles Dickens: An Introduction to His Novels*, K. J. Fielding's *Charles Dickens: A Critical Introduction*, Angus Wilson's *The World of Charles Dickens* (superbly illustrated with a number of color plates), and Harland S. Nelson's *Charles Dickens*. More specialized but useful as an introduction to Dickens and his works, Edmund Wilson's essay "Dickens: The Two Scrooges" introduces students to the serious side of Dickens and to many recurrent issues in modern Dickens criticism and biography.

Biographical Studies

Because *David Copperfield* draws so heavily upon events of Dickens' early life and had its germ in a fragment of autobiography preserved by his first biographer, teachers of the novel like to make John Forster's biography, *The Life of Charles Dickens*, available to their students. Forster's second chapter is based largely on Dickens' autobiography. Edgar Johnson's *Charles Dickens: His Tragedy and Triumph*, the standard modern biography, presents not only the background information about Dickens' childhood but also a full account of his many activities while writing *David Copperfield*. Edmund Wilson's essay serves many students as an incisive introduction to the relationship between Dickens' biography and novel. Too recently published to have found mention in the instructors' survey, Michael Slater's *Dickens and Women* provides a wealth of biographical and critical commentary about the women in Dickens' life, who figure so prominently in his presentation of Dora, Little Em'ly, and Agnes. More generally, Slater discriminates between fact and speculation as he takes into account what others have argued concerning Dickens' relationship with his mother, wife, and sister-in-law and with Ellen Ternan. So much recent critical commentary focuses on the relationship between fact and fiction, on the psychological issues of childhood remembered and of adulthood fantasized, and more broadly on the theoretical questions of autobiography, that instructors thinking of assigning biographical studies may first want to consult works mentioned below in The Instructor's Library.

Critical and Textual Studies

Of the many critical commentaries instructors suggest as helpful to students, a few recur with strong recommendations. J. Hillis Miller, in a chapter on the novel in his *Charles Dickens: The World of His Novels*, examines *David Copperfield* as both a novel of memory and a spiritual transcendence of personal misery. More directed toward a single theme, Gwendolyn Needham's "The Undisciplined Heart of David Copperfield" has given many readers insights about the book's meaning. Several teachers recommended that students contrast Needham's views with James Kincaid's more icono-clastic and provocative ideas in *Dickens and the Rhetoric of Laughter*. For an extensive critical discussion that regards *David Copperfield* as the apex of Dickens' achievement, students may consult Sylvère Monod's *Dickens the Novelist*. Students attracted by the book's use of fairy-tale devices and by its attention to the irrational should read the chapters on *David Copper-field* in Harry Stone's *Dickens and the Invisible World*. Teachers have been quick to recommend Bert Hornback's recent *"The Hero of My Life,"* which regards David's imagination as the novel's heroic element. For comparison of *David Copperfield* with *Great Expectations*, many instructors recom-mend the chapter on these novels in J.H. Buckley's study of the bildungs-roman, *Season of Youth*. For courses in which the genesis and monthly composition of the novel are subjects of interest, students definitely need to read John Butt's *"David Copperfield Month by Month"* in his and Kathleen Tillotson's *Dickens at Work*. An excellent and more recent discussion of the novel's compositional and textual history is available in Nina Burgis' intro-duction to the Clarendon *David Copperfield*. Students interested in the novel's illustrations should consult John Harvey's *Victorian Novels and Their Illustrators* and Michael Steig's *Dickens and Phiz*. For an account of the novel's reception and enduring popular and critical reputation, George H. Ford's *Dickens and His Readers* remains the standard work.

Other Dickens Works

Apart from assigned reading of other fiction by Dickens in courses that include more of his writing than *Copperfield*, several instructors recommend that undergraduates examine selected articles in *Household Words*, the weekly periodical Dickens began while writing *David Copperfield*. Articles of particular interest discuss Australian emigration, British schools, and various features of domestic life. For details, see Richard J. Dunn, *David Copperfield: An Annotated Bibliography*, entry 35. Teachers surveyed also occasionally recommend Dickens' Christmas books, especially *The Haunted Man* (1848), as useful for students interested in *David Copperfield*'s stress on memory.

Aids to Teaching

The subject of Dickens and film has attracted several recent critics, begin-ning with the famous Russian film director Sergei Eisenstein, who in a famous 1949 essay traced the influence of Dickens and the Victorian novel on D.W. Griffith and early American film (see also the essay by Melissa Sue

Kort in part 2). It is not surprising, therefore, that many Dickens novels, including *David Copperfield*, have received cinematic treatment.

The earliest film versions of *Copperfield* include an American abridgment in 1911; a 1913 British six-reeler, directed by Cecil Hepworth; and a 1922 Danish adaptation, directed by A.W. Sandberg. The most famous version is the 1935 MGM production, adapted by Hugh Walpole, directed by George Cukor, produced by David O. Selznick, and featuring W.C. Fields as Mr. Micawber, Basil Rathbone as Murdstone, Freddie Bartholomew as young David, and many other fine character actors. A 1970 film, directed by Delbert Mann, was produced by Omnibus–Twentieth Century Fox for television in the United States and for theatrical release in England. (See Zambrano's checklist, "Feature Motion Pictures" 108.)

None of these adaptations, however, succeeds in translating the novel's wealth onto the screen. The few teachers who use any of the film versions in class generally pointed out their shortcomings. The 1970 film, for example, is perhaps most notable for cameo appearances of many famous stage and screen stars (e.g., Michael Redgrave, Ralph Richardson, Laurence Olivier, Edith Evans, Richard Attenborough), and it so alters David into an existential searcher for the 1970s that it has seldom been used to accompany classroom study of the novel. The classic 1935 film is, of course, the most frequently shown but its wavering fidelity to the novel troubles some. As a reviewer of the film long ago remarked, it is often difficult to know whether W.C. Fields plays Micawber or Micawber plays Fields. This concern over fidelity seems to underlie most instructors' reluctance to show students the *Copperfield* films. One teacher finds "film too seductive in leading away from the text," though another, echoing Eisenstein, grants that the movie version helps us see Dickens' cinematic technique of narrative. Teachers who use the *Copperfield* films might wish to consult, among other works, A.L. Zambrano's *Dickens and Film* and essays by Gavin Lambert and William Luhr devoted to the 1935 adaptation. George Curry's screenplay for the 1970 version (*Copperfield '70*) was published by Ballantine.

Teachers of *David Copperfield* will also receive little assistance from recordings of the spoken word. Whereas readings as well as dramatizations of several other Dickens works have been recorded (e.g., *A Christmas Carol, Nicholas Nickleby, Oliver Twist, The Pickwick Papers, A Tale of Two Cities*), not a single recorded rendition of *David Copperfield* is available today.

Although responsible instructors would not consider various study guides as aids to teaching, they should be aware of materials students may purchase. Cliffs Notes and the Monarch guide are the most common in this country. In addition to the usual story synopsis and character sketches, J.M. Lybyer's Cliff Notes for *David Copperfield* summarize a number of general critical opinions without identifying the critics. The Monarch *Review Notes and*

Study Guide to Dickens' David Copperfield, which offers the dubious self-justification that it will help students better understand a work they "might otherwise have found hopelessly perplexing and therefore distasteful," does name several major critics and includes some informative commentary in its chapter summaries.

The Instructor's Library

The survey of Dickens teachers shows that the novel is taught in a variety of courses to students at different levels. It appears most often in courses on the novel and Dickens, as well as in courses on nineteenth-century and Victorian literature, fiction, narrative, and major British authors and more specialized classes on autobiographical writing, the bildungsroman, and Victorian culture. Therefore this checklist has two objectives: to present a guide to essential bibliographical, critical, and biographical studies for the teacher of Dickens and *David Copperfield* and also to note a number of studies that complement particular approaches and course contexts. With Dickens studies each year producing many books and dozens of articles, it is no surprise that the list of works instructors regard as helpful for their presentation runs to nearly one hundred. The following recommendations, which should be supplemented by other works mentioned in part 2, attempt to isolate essential works for present and prospective teachers of *David Copperfield*. Most of the cited works are books, many available in paperback, but a number of essays also are mentioned. The checklist is more descriptive than evaluative, and the mere presence of titles suggests that teachers have found them valuable.

Because *David Copperfield* has been regarded as pivotal in Dickens' career and as representative of both his strengths and his weaknesses as a writer, instructors may benefit from an awareness of the major directions in *Copperfield* criticism—and Dickens criticism in general—over the past century and a quarter. With few exceptions (Robert Garis, e.g., says little about *David Copperfield* in his reassessment of Dickens as a writer more prone to performance than to self-examination), the major Dickens critics have had a great deal to say about *David Copperfield*. In "*David Copperfield*: A Century of Critical and Popular Acclaim" Arthur Adrian traces the praise of those who find the novel free from earlier Dickensian excesses in its idealized version of personal history. This tradition of acclaim, however, has not prevented serious consideration of the novel by such commentators as H. A. Taine, who spoke of Dickens' hallucinatory imagination; G. K. Chesterton, who contends that Dickens takes illusion into account as a fact of life (*Charles Dickens*); and Edmund Wilson and J. Hillis Miller, who examine in more detail the biographical and philosophical implications of such imaginative activity.

The most comprehensive critical studies of *David Copperfield* outline the principal concerns of teachers and scholars: the novel's autobiographical nature, ambivalent attitude toward the hero, portrayal of childhood, combinations of realism and fantasy, psychological insights (especially about the act of remembering), and comedy. These studies also consider the novel's centrality to Dickens' career, reception by contemporaries, and influence on other writers, and recent works devote considerable attention to the first-person narration and the evocative and symbolic language.

Reference Works

The most useful general bibliographies for Dickens are in *Victorian Fiction: A Guide to Research*, edited by Lionel Stevenson, and *Victorian Fiction: A Second Guide to Research*, edited by George H. Ford. Ada Nisbet's bibliographic essay in the former, arranged by subject rather than by Dickens' individual works, is informative as a guide to Dickens studies and especially to Dickens' international reputation. Philip Collins, supplementing Nisbet in *A Second Guide*, changes some of her subject categories and adds sections for the individual novels. For a novel-by-novel guide to contemporary periodical criticism of Dickens, teachers should consult John J. Fenstermaker's *Charles Dickens, 1940–1975: An Analytical Subject Index to Periodical Criticism of the Novels and Christmas Books*. Fenstermaker cross-references articles concerned with characterization, characters, composition, critical assessment, explanatory notes, backgrounds and sources, illustrations, influences, language and style, literary parallels, plot, point of view, setting, structure/unity, techniques, text, and themes.

David Copperfield is the only Dickens novel for which there is a well-annotated bibliography of editions, adaptations, reviews, criticism, and appreciative and biographical commentary. Richard J. Dunn's David Copperfield: *An Annotated Bibliography* covers the years 1849–1980, has an author and subject index, and includes an introduction on the novel's popular and critical reception. Annotations describe—and, for the critical material, evaluate—the bibliography's 778 entries.

The three specialized publications on Dickens—the *Dickensian, Dickens Studies Newsletter* (after 1983 to appear as *Dickens Quarterly*), and *Dickens Studies Annual*—contain valuable bibliographic information on current scholarship: the *Dickensian* publishes reviews of all important editions and criticism and frequently surveys recent Dickens studies; the *Newsletter* also publishes reviews and maintains the most up-to-date quarterly checklist of editions, secondary studies, and miscellaneous items pertaining to

Dickens; and the *Annual* includes comprehensive review essays of recent major studies.

Text

The Clarendon edition of *David Copperfield*, which collates manuscript, proofs, and all editions published in Dickens' lifetime, has greatly simplified textual reference. This edition makes Dickens' number plans available in an appendix, and an excellent introduction by Nina Burgis discusses the genesis and composition of the novel. The textual notes in the Clarendon edition may satisfy most instructors' curiosity about the development of particular passages, but some might like to consult the full manuscript and proof. These are available on microfilm (*Manuscripts* and *Annotated Proofs*). The most complete study of the serial development appears in "*David Copperfield* Month by Month," in John Butt and Kathleen Tillotson's *Dickens at Work*. For a study of Dickens' relations with his publishers and for details about the early sales of *David Copperfield*, Robert Patten's *Dickens and His Publishers* is indispensable; for a thorough discussion of the illustrations, see Michael Steig's *Dickens and Phiz*.

Reception

As a discussion of the popular and critical reception and reputation of the novel and of Dickens in general, George H. Ford's *Dickens and His Readers* is essential. More generous samplings from early reviews and from other writers' comments about Dickens are available in Philip Collins' *Dickens: The Critical Heritage*, and the Dunn bibliography provides a chronological list and description of early reviews and of remarks by such writers as Carlyle, Thackeray, Browning, and Henry James. Dickens favored *Copperfield* in his public readings; the adapted reading text is included in Philip Collins' *Charles Dickens: The Public Readings*.

Biographies

Like those of many popular authors, Dickens' biography has become something of a public property. Even before his death in 1870 unauthorized and inaccurate biographies appeared, and in recent years biographical fictions as well as works claiming to hold important new revelations have been published. Teachers should base biographical study on Edgar Johnson's *Charles Dickens: His Tragedy and Triumph*. Johnson builds on John Forster's *The Life of Charles Dickens*, which contains all that remains of the autobiography Dickens attempts before starting *Copperfield*. The Dunn bibliography lists and annotates a number of more recent articles—centering on Dickens' childhood and his relationships with his family and with various women—that supplement Johnson's biographical work. Michael Slater has recently provided an indispensable study, *Dickens and Women*. In *The Forms of Autobiography: Episodes in the History of a Literary Genre*, William C. Spengemann not only discusses the novel's presentation of Dickens' life but also adds a brief bibliographical essay surveying other studies of the novel as autobiography.

Geographical studies of *David Copperfield*—in which locations are loaded with personal reference—are implicitly biographical studies and over the years many pages of the *Dickensian* have been devoted to discussion of the novel's settings. The most useful collected commentary is Michael and Mollie Hardwick's *Dickens's England*, for in their scrupulous attention to the actual places mentioned in *David Copperfield*, the Hardwicks recognize the imaginative values Dickens gives to places. Should an instructor have an opportunity to visit or to help students find what remains of the London Dickens described, Peter Roberson's *The London of Charles Dickens* can be helpful.

Critical Commentary

In addition to the valuable introductions to the Riverside and Penguin editions, there are several extensive commentaries on *David Copperfield*. Philip Collins' pamphlet *Charles Dickens:* David Copperfield appeared as part of a series designed to stimulate students' critical insights. Because it is hard to find in this country and is as useful for teachers as for students, it is mentioned here but not in the recommended student readings. Most libraries should have Sylvère Monod's *Dickens the Novelist*, which devotes nearly one hundred pages to *David Copperfield*. Monod's intelligent modern discussion of the novel considers its major themes and evaluates Dickens' method of presenting David as a character possessing a rich emotional life; and in *David Copperfield* Monod finds humor and serious psychology simultaneously present for the first time in Dickens. In a lengthy chapter on *David Copperfield* in *Dickens and the Invisible World*, Harry Stone presents the case for this novel as a primary example of Dickens' fairy-tale art. Readers interested in the book's mixtures of realism and fantasy might supplement Stone with more theoretical and general discussions of Dickens' art such as John Romano's *Dickens and Reality*, Robert Newsom's *Dickens on the Romantic Side of Familiar Things*, or John Kucich's *Excess and Restraint in Dickens*. Bert Hornback's *"The Hero of My Life"* takes *Copperfield* as the starting point for an eclectic critical study of Dickens as an artist whose goal was "the creation of human wisdom" (x). Hornback goes against the grain of commentary that criticizes *David Copperfield* for evading important personal and social issues, and, like G. K. Chesterton years earlier, he argues that for Dickens human happiness is the meaning of life. Hornback's title, drawn from the novel's opening sentence, signals his interest in the issue of David's heroism, a topic about which commentators have been divided. In *Charles Dickens: David Copperfield*, Philip Collins presents the view that David lacks complexity as both character and author. The most persuasive arguments for David's heroism are those of Hornback in "*The Hero of My Life*" and Robert B. Patten in "Autobiography into Autobiography: The Evolution of *David Copperfield*."

Consideration of *David Copperfield* as autobiographical fiction usually expands to a discussion of autobiography as both method and meaning. As method, autobiography involves setting boundaries between fact and fiction, selecting from and controlling memory, and skillfully presenting the first-person narrator. As meaning, autobiography assumes that a personal history can make sense and that memory can combine imagination and intelligence. Just what this novel may mean has been the subject of several studies. Gwendolyn Needham's influential essay "The Undisciplined Heart of David Copperfield" sees the principal concern to be the hero's largely successful struggle with himself. Taking a similar stance—though viewing David's struggle as less successful than Pip's in *Great Expectations*—J. H. Buckley in *Season of Youth* discusses *Copperfield* as a bildungsroman. In *Charles Dickens: The World of His Novels*, J. Hillis Miller considers *Copperfield* as a novel organized around complexities of romantic love and—an insight pursued by many subsequent critics—as primarily a novel of memory. Like Needham, Q. D. Leavis, in a chapter of *Dickens the Novelist*, argues that *David Copperfield* concerns the value of moral simplicity, and in a sound discussion of the Victorian idea of women and marriage, she concludes that the book's varied images of marriage provide no adequate answer to the question of happiness that Dickens posed.

Leavis assumes that *David Copperfield* is, as Tolstoy thought, a serious novel. However, many readers first enjoy the novel for its humor. Relatively few writers have attempted to discuss Dickens' humor at length, but the traditional enjoyment of it is perhaps best represented in G. K. Chesterton's *Charles Dickens*, where Chesterton responds positively to Dickensian exaggeration. John Carey's *The Violent Effigy* has a helpful chapter on Dickens' humor. Rejecting traditional views of both the novel's comedy and its primary concern with disciplining the heart, James Kincaid, in *Dickens and the Rhetoric of Laughter*, finds the humor subversive because of *David Copperfield*'s divided value systems.

Readers have never stopped arguing over the novel's picture of David's maturity, but there has been great praise for its presentation of childhood. Fine discussions of Dickens' use of children include John Carey's chapter in *The Violent Effigy* and Angus Wilson's "Dickens on Children and Childhood."

The evocation of earlier years by an adult narrator-protagonist under-standably raises readers' interest in the connection between memory and imagination. Commentators often recognize a kinship between Dickens and Wordsworth, Tennyson, or Charlotte Brontë in the self-conscious use of narrative memory. Carl Dawson devotes a chapter of his *Victorian Noon* to comparative study of "memory as a way of imagination that is at once retrospective and self-assertive" (124). More specifically focused on memory as a unifying force in the novel, Robin Gilmour's article remains one of the most lucid discussions of the function of memory in *David Copperfield*. Ranging further through Dickens, Barry Westburg's *The Confessional Fictions of Charles Dickens* treats the topic at length, and Robert Lougy, in an essay called "Remembrances of Death Past and Future: A Reading of *David Copperfield*," speculates about the potential for self-deception that arises in a book structured as a remembering and a forgetting.

Among studies of narrative method, Harvey P. Sucksmith's *The Narrative Art of Charles Dickens* frequently mentions *David Copperfield* but does not give it a separate section. Felicity Hughes's essay "Narrative Complexity in *David Copperfield*" argues that the book's varied perspectives of the young David, David the narrator, and David the man qualify one another. The present-tense "Retrospect" chapters have inspired much discussion; George H. Ford's "Dickens and the Voices of Time" treats them as an example of a developing private prose style.

Teachers of *David Copperfield*—and for that matter of any Dickens novel—should be able to answer students' questions concerning Dickens' methods of characterization. The already mentioned studies of the novel's autobiographical quality and the presentation of its narrator-hero have obvious relevance to its characterization, as do G. K. Chesterton's comments on Dickens' methods of exaggeration for comic effect (*Charles Dickens*). Harry Stone provides a useful discussion of how the book's fairy-tale elements contribute to the psychological realism of the characterization (*Invisible World*). The classic definition of Dickens' characterization, however, appears in E. M. Forster's *Aspects of the Novel*; in describing differences between round and flat characterizations, Forster often mentions Dickens and *David Copperfield*.

The particular demands that a Dickens novel makes on readers often reflect a style and publication format with which modern readers have little familiarity. The expansive, often excessive rhetoric of melodrama is well explained by George Worth in *Dickensian Melodrama*; the special demands of serial publication receive close attention from Butt and Tillotson (*Dickens at Work*) and from Archibald C. Coolidge, Jr. (*Charles Dickens as Serial Novelist*). More recently, Susan Horton in *The Reader in the Dickens World* argues that Dickens reconciled conflicts between audience demands and his own attitudes toward personal and public issues by varying his modes of presentation. Harland S. Nelson's study includes chapters on Dickens' relations with his audience and on his serial form of publication.

It may be helpful, in conclusion, to report what one instructor suggested as most valuable for anyone preparing to teach the novel for the first time. He listed resources with the sensible reminder that many secondary works that "enrich our understanding of *David Copperfield* employ similar factual materials, textual citations, and critical approaches" and therefore no single reference may be essential. His choices are Edgar Johnson's critical chapter in *Charles Dickens: His Tragedy and Triumph* (deleted from the 1977 abridged edition); George H. Ford's introduction to the Riverside edition; Richard J. Dunn's article "*David Copperfield*: All Dickens Is There"; Gwendolyn Needham's essay "The Undisciplined Heart of David Copperfield"; and the *Copperfield* chapters in J. Hillis Miller's *Charles Dickens: The World of His Novels*, Harry Stone's *Charles Dickens and the Invisible World*, and John Lucas' *The Melancholy Man: A Study of Dickens's Novels*. The person who suggested these works commented:

> Although some Dickensians have disparaged Johnson's critical chapters, I find these stimulating and useful in defining major issues; Needham's article and Miller's comments appear to have influenced many later studies of *David Copperfield*, while the essays by Ford and Dunn seem effective in providing general introductions to the novel. The chapters by Stone and Lucas present approaches that I believe are especially attractive to undergraduates.

Part Two

APPROACHES

INTRODUCTION

The following essays by teachers of *David Copperfield* are arranged in two sections: general discussions of teaching the novel as a central part of various literature classes and explanations of specific teaching approaches. The authors represent a range of experience; they teach at universities, colleges, and community colleges in the United States and Canada. Some have published often on Dickens, and, unaware of whose contributions would appear with theirs, the authors have freely cited one another's previous work. Clearly, no single approach is definitive in teaching a novel read and taught in as many contexts as is *David Copperfield*, but in these articles one may note a few recurrent questions about teaching Dickens and about the choice of *David Copperfield* as a text.

Just as literary criticism once found ways to dismiss Dickens as a popular but not serious writer, so, too, did some teachers relegate him to the public-library shelves, book-discussion groups, and secondary-school classrooms. The past thirty years have brought Dickens into more kinds of college and university classes, but even when conducting the survey of teachers for this volume, I received several responses declaring *Copperfield* a novel for adolescents, not appropriate for study at the college level, and at best one of Dickens' lesser productions. Not having surveyed secondary teachers, I cannot estimate how often they teach the novel, but over the years my own university students have reported reading *A Tale of Two Cities*, *Hard Times*, *Great Expectations*, or *Oliver Twist*, if they have read any Dickens at all before entering college. As for the complaint that this is not Dickens' best novel, we need to realize how measures of relative excellence vary according to which Dickens we are considering. One tradition of Dickens criticism and pedagogy regards *Copperfield* as the last and somewhat disappointing example of his youthful comic energies. Another view perceives it as not fitting the pattern of Dickens' career in the later 1840s and early 1850s, because as nostalgic self-scrutiny *David Copperfield* seems to ignore social issues that Dickens had stressed in *Dombey and Son* and would return to in *Bleak House*. Yet another view regrets the book's lack of integrity and coherence; the early parts are fine—as Edgar Johnson has said, "All childhood is there" (691)—but the older David is a bore, and his story may lack the ironic intelligence of Pip's in *Great Expectations*.

This is not the place for lengthy discussion of these issues, but it should be evident that each challenge to *Copperfield* may present as much reason to teach as not to teach the novel. Certainly we must confront Dickens' comic vision: is it amiable, grotesque, possibly subversive? And in a novel so intimately autobiographical, just what is the reflective narration concentrating on in David's life? Granted, *David Copperfield* does not anatomize society as satirically or symbolically as does *Bleak House*, but in raising questions of heroism, showing strained relationships among family members, and feeling the impact of religious discipline, it addresses significant social concerns. Moreover, its blend of fact and fiction challenges teachers and students to participate in the process of imaginative recollection. As many of the following essays show, formal study of *David Copperfield* demands attention to its patterns of repetition, theme and character development, and sustained moods and motifs. Such approaches do not ignore flaws in the artistry, inadequacies in the conception, but simply insist that readers see as Dickens (and often David) saw. Thus, however one stands on the book's overall quality, one seems obliged to recognize that in addition to being a classic work of fiction, *David Copperfield* is both a representative and a pivotal Dickens work.

The section of general discussions begins with Daniel Sheridan's "*David Copperfield*: Different Readers, Different Approaches." Sheridan's view, based on many years of teaching the book to three types of literature students (sophomores, upper-division majors, and graduate students), grants the individuality of any single class as well as the recurrence of certain issues but recognizes that the different levels of students may benefit from different approaches in the classroom. In "*Copperfield* on Trial: Meeting the Opposition," Susan J. Hanna describes her methods of engaging students with the text to develop their critical abilities and of approaching the novel through objections to it (and to much Victorian fiction). Thomas M. Leitch in "Dickens' Problem Child" discusses problems of teaching a novel that is both a popular classic and a writer's most autobiographical work. He grants that there are common problems to interest both pedagogy and criticism but argues that "what are problems for the critic become opportunities for the teacher, whose primary aim is to provoke rather than to resolve discussion."

Beverly Lyon Clark comments on teaching *David Copperfield* in a children's literature course, and all instructors of *David Copperfield* may benefit from her approach to it as a work both representing and challenging views of childhood. More traditionally, Margaret Scanlan assigns *Copperfield* in her introduction to fiction course, and her essay centers on how she expects this novel to give students a sense of the traditional novel and an opportunity to confront the moral and political issues it raises.

It is a commonplace of modern criticism to speak of Dickens in connection with Tolstoy, Dostoevsky, or Kafka, and *David Copperfield* fits well into many world and comparative literature courses. Willis Konick, in "The Chords of Memory: Teaching *David Copperfield* in the Context of World Literature," outlines a way to teach the novel with others (ranging from works of Dostoevsky to those of Céline) in which the force of childhood memory predominates. Similarly concerned with thematic comparisons, Gerhard Joseph discusses his course that centers on patterns of confessional self-revelation in Victorian nonfictional and fictional prose. In "Fathers and Sons: *David Copperfield* in a Course on Victorian Autobiographical Prose," Joseph characterizes his pedagogy as eclectic, psychoanalytic, and theoretical.

Instructors offer various approaches to the problem of accommodating the sheer bulk of *Copperfield* to a course calendar. Stanley Friedman writes about using the novel to introduce a Dickens course that requires reading at least six long novels. To accustom his students to the pace of the Dickens novel, Friedman divides the text into nine assignments, stressing throughout the autobiographical elements of this book published at the midpoint of Dickens' writing life.

The second part, Specific Approaches, contains essays that directly concern methods of teaching instead of describing courses that use the novel. The first two, however, discuss the usefulness of *Copperfield* in creative and expository writing instruction. Jean Ferguson Carr, in "David Copperfield's 'Written Memory,' " indicates the kinds of autobiographical writing her teaching of the novel stimulates, and Melissa Kort, in " 'I have taken with fear and trembling to authorship': *David Copperfield* in the Composition Classroom," speaks of Dickens as an embodiment of what is good and bad in writing.

For all the wealth of background and secondary reading on Dickens and *David Copperfield* few teachers have found ways of involving undergraduates directly beyond the text, but in "*David Copperfield*: Parallel Reading for Undergraduates," J. Gill Holland shows how, through journal assignments, he has encouraged additional reading and enriched discussion.

Three essays suggest strategies for dealing with *David Copperfield*'s long serial format. George Worth, in *"Multum in Parvo*: The Ninth Chapter of *David Copperfield*," offers a method for concentrated study once students have completed their reading. Michael Lund, in "Testing by Installments the 'Undisciplined Heart' of *David Copperfield*'s Reader," describes assignments that simulate the original reading experience. Lund finds that this approach helps his students see how the book's "form insists on maturity from its readers." With a pedagogy she terms "psychoanalytic, poststructuralist, feminist," Dianne F. Sadoff provides a day-by-day account of her discussion-oriented effort to bring a class to terms with as much as possible of *David Copperfield*.

The volume's final two essays, Susan R. Horton's "Making Sense of *David Copperfield*" and Michael Steig's *"David Copperfield* and Shared Reader Response," complement one another even though they were conceived and written independently. Horton focuses on her strategies for maintaining "an honest discussion of the situation of interpretation" that respects the variety of shapes and colors she and her students see in *David Copperfield* as they make sense of it. Steig, in a report of "a teaching method in progress," acknowledges the influence of Norman Holland and David Bleich but warns that the pedagogy he has adopted "must be shaped by every teacher to his or her teaching personality and abilities." For the prospective teacher uncertain about the substance of a response pedagogy that must remain so flexible, Horton provides a detailed sample of her classroom response to *David Copperfield*, and Steig documents his students' writing and discussion. The encouragement these teachers give others to "go and do likewise" applies not simply to the objective of reader-response teaching but more generally to the purpose of this volume: to share views of how best to bring *David Copperfield* into classroom instruction.

RJD

GENERAL DISCUSSIONS

David Copperfield: Different Readers, Different Approaches

Daniel Sheridan

Nearly every year I manage to work *David Copperfield* into my teaching schedule, sometimes with sophomore nonmajors, at times with junior and senior English majors, and occasionally with graduate students. Each time around our approach to the novel varies a little, as do our activities in the classroom. Many of the differences, of course, reflect the idiosyncrasies of this or that group of students and thus defy classification. But others—the ones that concern me here—reflect consistent differences between grade levels and thus can be both classified and predicted. Whether these variations are teacher-generated (resulting, say, from shifts in my teaching objectives) or student-generated (resulting from differences in the reading habits of students on various levels) is an open question; as the following remarks suggest, I'm inclined to see the two as inseparable. In any case my purpose is not to analyze the causes but to describe the differences themselves. I'd like, therefore, to examine a general approach to *Copperfield* for each level, commenting on student responses to the novel and outlining some of the classroom techniques that have worked best with each group. In focusing on what is typical of a given level, I will no doubt neglect important individual differences among students and significant similarities between levels. Still, the general distinctions seem valid: my experience suggests that the three groups—sophomores, upper-division majors, and graduate students—read the novel in different ways and thus benefit from different approaches in the classroom.

My sophomores are always nonmajors, a mixed group of students from such fields as engineering, nursing, and business. Usually these students, although bright, have had little experience with literature, particularly with serious fiction longer than *The Old Man and the Sea*. One reason for assigning *Copperfield*, then, is to initiate them into the joys and complexities of a long novel, in the process helping them understand their own reading habits. In one experimental effort I tried teaching *Copperfield* as the only text in a five-week minicourse, but under any circumstances I like to leave as much time as possible for students to savor the novel and analyze their reading. This leisurely pace emphasizes the act of reading—that is, the interaction between reader and text. We spend time discussing student predictions about the course of the story (usually at the end of class) and the way the text confirms or alters those predictions (normally at the start of the next class). Moreover, this emphasis on reader responses and predictions allows us to focus on the rhetoric of the fiction. What begins as a sort of guessing game, though by no means a random one, soon becomes a collective discussion of the way the novel's language and structure shape predictions and determine the rhetoric of reading.

This approach has much in common with high school teaching, where course content is not predetermined but is derived from analyzing what students think and feel as they read. I keep background material to a minimum at first, because the personal backgrounds that students bring to the text have a greater influence on their reading of *Copperfield* than does a few hours' lecture on Dickens or Victorian England. We get to the historical material later, but we begin with the first sentence of the novel and with students' expectations of a book that starts as *Copperfield* does. This leads to a discussion of heroism (will David be the hero of his own life?), which students tend to describe as positive, decisive activity. That their heroes are all doers, people who change their worlds in some way, has much to do with students' later reactions to the protagonist. And we explore their reactions to an adult narrator who feels compelled to begin the story of his own development in this tentative, half-apologetic manner. Students are clearly interested in the psychology of growing up, predicting immediately that the story will deal with the relation between heroism (as they define it) and maturity. The first class then concludes with a reading of chapter 1 and a call for predictions, to be written down and brought to the next class.

These sophomores tend to read *Copperfield* in a linear fashion, paying more attention to the protagonist's forward movement than to the backward perspective, and shaping influence, of the narrator. It helps, then, to focus on point of view early in the course, examining the devices Dickens uses to distinguish the adult narrator from the developing child: the visual perspective of a small child, the shift in language from the specific to the general in the "Retrospect" chapters, and the fairy-tale elements of the early sections, which create a sense of distance between the two Davids. We are likely, for example, to spend some time discussing fairy tales and establishing connections between their stock characters and characters in the novel—the prince, princess, fairy godmother, witch, troll, faithful servant. This attention to fairy tale fits in well with students' interest in developmental psychology (many are taking introductory psychology courses at the same time) and in turn provides a natural bridge to the ideas of security and risk taking that are so important in the bildungsroman. And when some students give us the inevitable oedipal reading of David's childhood, we can start to analyze the function of women in *Copperfield*, the roles they play not just in David's life but in the larger Victorian scene.

Ironically, then, the analysis of fairy-tale motifs, which appeals to students' psychological and essentially ahistorical approach, gets us into the social dimensions of the novel. For once we begin to talk about the young David as a disinherited prince, we must address the question of his inheritance—his place in the Victorian middle class, as well as the rewards and values of that class. In making that transition, we find Uriah Heep an important character. The moment he appears as "a cadaverous face" at the window of a "little round tower" in the Wickfield home (ch.15), he is identified as the villain of the piece, the sorcerer, monster, or troll who lurks at the bottom of things. Uriah is the troll under the bridge, but he sheds light on the bridge itself, on the way it spans social classes. As our focus shifts from "growing up" in general to "being and becoming middle-class in Victorian England," students begin to understand certain aspects of David's character: his fear of falling from middle-class grace, his failure to act when his class affiliation seems to be at stake, and his poorly concealed competition with Uriah for possession of Agnes. It is important, I think, for students to appreciate Uriah's view of the Victorian scene, even if I must play devil's advocate and argue his case. Only then can they temper their sympathy for David with a more critical attitude, coming to terms with their growing sense that he will never quite measure up to their notions of heroism.

Discussions of Uriah help us move from the general to the particular, from the mythic to the historical. I take up social issues—class divisions, education and the work ethic, the family, and the status of women—on an ad hoc basis, in response to questions that arise as we predict and interpret. This inductive approach is often time-consuming and not always efficient, but it has distinct advantages: it addresses the social implications of *Copperfield* without resorting to the tacked-on lecture, the bane of so many English courses, and it helps place the burden of synthesis where it belongs—on the students themselves. In this connection, it's useful to have students put as much in writing as possible. Short exercises, sometimes just worksheets to fill out, serve as homework and as the basis for small-group activities: comparisons of the active and passive verbs in key passages (those in which David is called on to act); lists of the names assigned to the young David, to get at the question of his proper identity; time lines of the plot, which record the stages of his development; connections to famous fairy tales; groups of character types, especially among the women. Short compositions—a fairy-tale version of the plot, for example, or the outline of a paper on the meaning of work or the roles of women—serve the double function of brief, in-class reports and drafts of longer, final papers. These exercises keep our discussions concrete and help students clarify their ideas.

My classes with sophomores initially emphasize rhetoric and the reading process, but those with junior and senior English majors focus directly and immediately on social history. In both genre surveys and period courses, my approach is essentially sociological—less concerned with literary history, in fact, than with the social circumstances of Victorian England and the status of the text as a historical document. This attention to history, as well as to the critical issues that arise from history, is appropriate to an undergraduate course for majors and has an important effect on what happens in the classroom. For example, much as I try to hold onto the positive features of the lower-division couses—the relaxed time schedule, the attention to reading, the frequent writing assignments and in-class activities—we are obliged to read more quickly and to discuss the novel in a large group. Moreover, students approach the act of reading differently, perhaps because treating *Copperfield* as a social document tends to "freeze" it, placing the emphasis on the whole, the product, rather than the process.

The emphasis of the course, then, helps explain why upper-division students react to David so differently, why they are more inclined to remain detached and to criticize his behavior as middle-class hero. *Copperfield* is often the first novel we read, and they bring to it discussions of other nonfictional texts—chiefly Carlyle and Mill—that have fixed their attention on the climate of the age and the central position of the middle class in Victorian culture. They are thus more likely than the sophomores to focus on David's circumstances, on his world rather than himself. We tend to discuss sociological, historical, or political topics: the family, child rearing, domestic arrangements, education, careers, finances, sexual attitudes, prostitution, and class structure. We do not ignore David; rather, in our handling of the dynamics of the bildungsroman, we give more attention to the shaping influence of the larger society than to the individual who interacts with it.

Students' sense of detachment from the protagonist also reflects their greater sensitivity to the nuances of the first-person point of view. The fairy-tale elements, for example, which serve as an important structuring device for the sophomores, take on the added dimension of irony. To the extent that students see these devices as a child's exaggeration, they take

David less seriously, even in his portrayal of the Murdstones and particularly in the London scenes. This insight injects a note of irony into their reading, at first through a sense of disjunction between the child and the adult narrator and later—once the two visions of David have started to blend— through a feeling of disparity between their view of David and his attitude toward himself. Why, they are inclined to ask, is the narrator so intent on eliciting our sympathy when he is so obviously telling his story from the standpoint of a successful Victorian gentleman? Does he understand all the implications of the choices he has made? These are questions that I have to raise with the sophomores; the juniors and seniors get there more quickly, on their own.

By posing the questions this way—that is, by emphasizing success instead of heroism—upper-division students reveal their concern with the social context of David's story. They are particularly interested in Dickens' handling of the female characters, not just in relation to David's growth but as Victorian types. Thus we take pains to examine the different kinds of women, grouping them according to various principles: sexual and non-sexual; upper-, middle-, and lower-class; domestic and enterprising; assertive and subservient. We then compare the resulting categories to what we know about Victorian women from other sources, both literary and historical. This process leads not only to a greater understanding of how Dickens uses and transforms social reality but also to a fuller, more detailed analysis of the function of women within the novel. For example, we explore minor characters and subplots, which in the sophomore classes receive only glancing attention, in some depth: Mrs. Gummidge, Mrs. Micawber, Miss Mowcher, and Martha; the stories of Rosa Dartle and Annie Strong. The central issue, of course, is power—the distribution of power between men and women and the struggle for power between characters of the same sex—and this topic leads us, inevitably, back to David. We can now analyze his ambivalent attitudes toward women (the way he alternately submits to and dominates the women of his life) and the more general issue of his power to control his own life.

There remains, however, the problem of irony and its relation to the narrator's stance and Dickens' intent. Here Uriah is once again an important character, for students' reactions to him most clearly reveal their critical biases. Some, for instance, opt for a straight reading, either sharing or rejecting the narrator's revulsion but in any case accepting his view as the author's. Others point out that Uriah functions as a foil for David and that, like all foils, he is in a sense a mirror—in this case, a character who both exploits and reveals the hidden feelings and values of middle-class people like David. In recognizing Uriah's ability to bring David's fears and desires to the surface (his uneasy sense of his own position, his fear of being identified as lower-class, his suspicions of Annie Strong), students reveal their distrust of the narrator and continue to read ironically. The source of the irony then becomes the topic of our final discussions: is it based in the text, or is it a creation of the reader, a "revision" of the text? Inevitably, the issue of intent will surface—as it must in discussions that attempt to relate literature to social history.

As the previous comments suggest, these classes emphasize discussion and debate. This is partly due to the tight reading schedule, for we are always pressed for time, and discussion remains the shortest route to the central issues. Of course, we have some other activities: small-group sessions based on worksheets (especially for analyzing the female characters), a great deal of oral reading (for language analysis), and some role playing (to alter perspectives on different characters). But mostly we discuss the issues and problems. For my part, I try to maintain a balance between moderating and participating, often signaling a shift in my role by handing over the reins to a student and even moving to occupy that student's desk. Though this practice might seem overly formal, it allows me to move in and out of debates without confusing my roles, thus avoiding the problem of the hidden agenda—the tendency to deliver a lecture while pretending to act only as moderator. But because the issues are clear and concrete and because students enjoy *Copperfield*, they participate eagerly and keep me in my place.

Time pressure and the consequent constraints on discussion are even more serious in graduate courses, where we might have only one or two three-hour sessions to cover *Copperfield*. So we limit objectives, abandoning any attempt to examine the rhetoric of the novel in detail or to do more than sketch its social dimensions—one likes to think that these activities are less necessary in graduate courses (a delusion, perhaps). Thus we move quickly to evaluate the novel in relation to Dickens' other work. The breadth of our comparison, of course, depends entirely on the class: in a Dickens seminar we will read seven or eight other novels, whereas in a more general course our only Dickensian point of reference might be *Great Expectations*. Because the latter situation is common and because of the obvious connections between the two novels, the following comments focus on our efforts to compare *Copperfield* to *Great Expectations* though any (or all) of the later novels could function in the same way.

This emphasis on evaluation through comparison obviously changes the approach one takes to *Copperfield* in a graduate class. Discussions of the novel always have a tentative quality, for we know that *Great Expectations*, which many have already read, is to follow. It is useless to pretend that students will not read *Copperfield* in the light of the later work, with a sort of comparative bias—usually unfavorable to *Copperfield*. What is most important, I think, is to delay judgment as we raise the critical issues and problems. Postponement is not always easy, but it is well worth the attempt, for we often have our most productive discussions of *Copperfield* later in the course, when we are reading *Great Expectations.* It is therefore important to instill in the class a wait-and-see attitude—which calls for some delaying tactics on my part and a good deal of on-the-spot coordination of classroom activities.

The question of secondary or collateral readings is relevant here. With the sophomores I let *Copperfield* stand on its own, providing any historical or critical commentary myself, and in the upper-level undergraduate classes we read only a few short pieces in addition to the novel itself: selections from Edgar Johnson's biography, a sampling of contemporary reviews, and one essay—usually either George Orwell or Edmund Wilson. Graduate students, however, should read more of the biography, more reviews, and both Orwell and Wilson. I am also likely to assign one or two critical essays (chosen from popular collections) or chapters from books on Dickens, yet I am reluctant to select them in advance. To fix on a particular piece—Barbara Hardy on "change of heart," for example, or Dorothy Van Ghent on "the Dickens world"—is sometimes tempting, but it always seems better to wait. For after all, class discussions, which provide clues to students' interests and critical vocabulary, are a better guide to choosing secondary readings. And, in any case, I prefer to adapt these readings to the discussions rather than vice versa.

I tend to take the same attitude toward seminar reports. Each student writes at least one short paper, based on some extra reading, and then adapts it for an in-class report. They may choose topics from a list I provide or follow their own interests, but they must develop an argument (not just report on their reading) and relate it to class discussions. And there lies the rub. It helps, I've found, to separate the paper from the report, for if I comment on the paper first I can help the student modify it for class presentation. I have a limited tolerance for rambling, off-the-cuff reports, and I also want the report to pursue an issue that arose in class. If we must postpone a report, then so be it, but we seldom have to do that if students have chosen the secondary reading with care. Normally, reports on other Dickens novels (preferably early ones) and on Dickens' life are easy to integrate into discussions of *Copperfield.* Since I prefer to take a wait-and-see approach to evaluating the novel, I tend to delay reports on the literary criticism.

Student reactions to *Copperfield* on this first go-round are decidedly mixed. They admit that the novel is "a good read" and delight in the versatility of the language and the handling of first-person narration in the childhood scenes. But their criticisms of the whole are often harsh. Perhaps because of the breakneck reading schedule, our attention focuses on the later sections—the marriage to Dora, the Uriah intrigue, the gradual movement toward union with Agnes—and poor David does not fare well.

Like the juniors and seniors, graduate students object to the treatment of women—especially to David's way of patronizing Dora and canonizing Agnes—but this objection is now subsumed under more general criticism of David's class attitudes: the worship of Steerforth, the inability to accept his complicity in the Peggottys' troubles, the extremity of his reaction to Uriah, the part he plays (or fails to play) in the Annie Strong plot. Even their response to David's homelessness is unsympathetic: they see it as a result of his being middle-class and not knowing exactly what that entails. To paraphrase one student, David is never at home because he's never at ease with himself, "always slumming or hobnobbing without even knowing it."

That phrase—"without even knowing it"—represents the gist of students' criticism. *Copperfield*, they say, sails along nicely until the reader begins to identify the protagonist with the adult narrator. At that point, which occurs as early as the first "Retrospect" chapter, thematic inconsistencies develop, and neither the narrator nor Dickens seems aware of legitimate objections to David's attitudes and behavior. For unlike the undergraduates, these students sense little irony at work in the narrative. They are impatient with the suggestion that the narrator might be unreliable, arguing that Dickens fails to provide within the text a means for disassociating oneself from the narrator's stance. Their reaction to Uriah is typical in this respect: instead of providing the reader with a new perspective on David, Dickens cops out and makes Uriah a scapegoat. Thus they argue that the adult David's lack of self-awareness prevents Dickens from exploring the central theme of the bildungsroman: the hero's progress, through conflict with the larger society, toward a mature understanding of the balance of power between himself and his environment.

This reading has much to recommend it. Harsh as it might seem, it allows us to discuss the social context, the language and tone of the narration, and the novel's place in the history of the bildungsroman. Nor am I inclined to challenge its validity. But there are problems here, not the least of which is the dubious distinction between "a good read" and "a good novel" implied by many student comments. Thus I suggest, rather mildly, that this assessment evades an important question, that readability is itself an aesthetic concern inseparable from issues of theme and structure. Hasty conclusions about Dickens' intent also make me uneasy. Without denying that the author was indeed caught up in his hero's values and dilemmas, I urge students to consider how much their interpretation depends on information about Dickens' life and about the autobiographical beginnings of the novel. Finally, I'm likely to challenge their definition of the bildungsroman, asking whether that ingredient of self-understanding is essential. On the whole, these are simply delaying tactics, but they keep certain issues—like the idea of irony—alive for the moment.

Our discussions of *Copperfield* in connection with *Great Expectations* serve not so much to change students' minds as to clarify their initial criticism. We begin by noting obvious similarities between the texts: the use of first-person point of view; the description of a child who struggles to come to terms with his world; the emphasis on loss, leave-taking, and death; the link between homelessness and an ambivalent sense of one's social class. Some of the differences are equally obvious: Pip's origin in the working class; his heightened sense of aloneness and vulnerability; and the theme of unresolved—perhaps undeserved—guilt that permeates *Great Expectations*. Indeed, our discussions of the later work focus on Dickens' handling of the paradox of guilt—Pip's growing sense that he is, in fact, guilty in spite of his ignorance and lack of genuine power.

Yet even here, at what seems the point of greatest difference between the two novels, we can explore the possibility of close connections. For example, the question of irony in *Copperfield* resurfaces, this time in a new context. For if in the later work Dickens treats guilt as a universal condition and examines the ironic relation between power and responsibility, is it legitimate to approach David's story in the same way? Perhaps not, as adherents of New Criticism respond, but the question is still productive. They must at least address a related question: when we see a connection between regret and guilt, between David's nostalgic romanticism and Pip's more thorough alienation from the forge, are we talking about a difference in kind or in degree? This approach leads to a sense that David achieves success at some cost. And by comparing the way class divisions are handled in the two novels, students realize that *Copperfield* is tougher and more insightful than they might first have believed. Whatever the problems with David himself, other characters compare favorably with those in *Great Expectations*: Steerforth (versus Bentley Drummle) as the upper-class Barbarian, the Micawbers (versus the Pockets) as representatives of middle-class pretensions, Uriah (versus Magwitch) as a type for the struggling underclass. True to form, Uriah plays his part in discussion. Even as we note the absence of such a villain in *Great Expectations* (Orlick simply won't do) and examine the significance of this void (Pip has no one to slap but himself), we can see that Uriah is more than a scapegoat. He is also a stroke of genius: a catalyst for action, a forcer of issues, a mirror for examining the middle-class hero.

My purpose is not to convince students that *Copperfield* is as "good" as *Great Expectations* but to broaden their perspective and challenge some critical assumptions. One such assumption is that because *Copperfield* is a bildungsroman, it must stand or fall on the question of the protagonist's self-awareness. This issue is relevant, of course—as the comparison to *Great Expectation* reveals—but students must examine the idea of the bildungsroman instead of treating it as a fixed label. We can also reexamine the idea that the autobiographical impulse behind *Copperfield* is somehow, in itself, the cause of problems in the narration. There is a defensible argument here, but it is hardly a valid assumption, especially in light of *Great Expectations* (which stems from the same impulse) and the general continuity of Dickens' work. And, finally, those assumptions about high and low art, about "good reads" and "good novels," never adequately explain the way effective fiction works. This last issue forces the question of standards out into the open, allowing us to discuss—in this concrete instance—what makes a successful novel. Of course, the chips must fall where they may—students might conclude that *Copperfield* is neither a good read nor a good novel, but they must base their evaluation on some theory of fiction. In fact, few students reach this conclusion; more often, they come to a greater appreciation and understanding of *Copperfield's* success as a work of art.

I am aware that in the previous comments, especially those on my graduate classes, I have devoted almost as much attention to *Copperfield's* problems and defects as to its strengths. On the one hand, this emphasis is unfortunate, not just because I consider it a great novel but because I am aware that negative teaching—assigning a work in order to pick at it or compare it unfavorably to other literature—is never productive. When we ask students to read a novel, especially one as long as *Copperfield,* we should believe it to be worth reading in itself. Whether or not *Copperfield* is as great a novel as *Little Dorrit* or *Great Expectations*—or *Jane Eyre, Vanity Fair, Middlemarch,* or any other—is a question more relevant to cocktail party conversation than to the classroom. On the other hand, standards are relevant, and comparative analysis is not necessarily shallow or invidious. So unless we are willing to relegate *Copperfield* to the lifeless status of a classic, teaching it only to admire it, we must take a critical stance, neither selling nor debunking it but taking it for what it is.

I think *Copperfield* is a great—though flawed—novel. Our reasons for assigning it are many and varied—helping students become better readers, introducing them to the complexities of Victorian society, giving them a sense of Dickens' place in the development of the modern novel—but regardless of the approach we teach it, ultimately, for its strengths and weaknesses. Indeed, we might go further and say that our teaching is effective precisely insofar as we encourage students to explore those strengths and weaknesses. Otherwise, we wind up praising the novel uncritically or apologizing for having asked students to read it in he first place. And *David Copperfield* does not need our apologies. It fares well in the classroom, even when subjected to the most penetrating criticism, continuing to reward us as we encounter it anew with different groups of readers.

Copperfield on Trial: Meeting the Opposition

Susan J. Hanna

A special pleasure of teaching *David Copperfield* is that it sells itself so effectively. In a Victorian literature course, I expect to spend a considerable amount of time leading students to appreciate the strange Victorian modes of expression, but the rhetoric in *Copperfield*, no matter how unfamiliar, never seems to interfere with the enjoyment. Few students have read the book before they enter the class, few have seen the movie or the television adaptation, but even those biased against long Victorian novels find their prejudices melting before Betsey Trotwood has stalked her way out of Blunderstone Rookery, and for most the interest holds straight through to page 669 (Riverside edition). The teacher's task, then, is not to overcome students' suspicion of those strange Victorians but the more pleasant one of helping them appreciate the art of a text already enjoyed.

A more pleasant task, but not an easy one. If we impose too orderly an analysis we feel like Murdstone. However, if we structure our investigation too loosely we run the danger that we'll all go meandering, lost in the complexities of the book's great length and rich texture, and finding especially good spots, like mushrooms in a forest, to hold up for general approval.

One useful structure that provides just enough framework to keep the discussion from wandering, exploits the students' own critical abilities, and focuses the investigation on the text is to approach the book through objections to it. I provide the objection; the class provides evidence for and against it. We carefully avoid coming to a final conclusion, at least as a class; one issue will appear as a major essay question in the final examination, where individuals may reach all the conclusions they wish.

The objections must be reasonable and supportable—this is no exercise in "get the critic" (a technique wisely disparaged in a previous volume in this series). I usually begin with a specific well-phrased quotation and then try to summarize related criticisms. Objections must not be idiosyncratic; instead, they should represent a school or an era. Students who write their term papers on Dickens find that they have, in a general way, already met issues central to critical attitudes toward Dickens. Finally, the issues chosen must send the student to the text of the novel rather than to biography or historical background.

I open discussion of the book by bringing up about three or four objections—not more, because if carried on too long the technique may become a game. This plan depends on the students' having finished the entire book—I haven't experimented yet with adapting it to the "reading in parts" plan described elsewhere in this book.

There is no difficulty finding intelligent objections to *Copperfield*, for perhaps no Dickens book has brought such fervent, even bad-tempered, complaints from readers, including those who admit to having enjoyed it for years. (In fact, those who most readily admit to having enjoyed it for years are often those who attack *Copperfield* most fiercely, with the sense that they have been somehow betrayed.) To open discussion, I look for a debate that will best give the students a grasp of the book as a whole. This is, undoubtedly, the objection that the book lacks shape: it is disorganized, it breaks into two parts; it may move organically and masterfully for a hundred pages through David's childhood but then lurches from episode to episode. I may summarize in David Cecil's words:

> [Dickens] cannot construct, for one thing. His books have no organic unity; they are full of detachable episodes, characters who serve no purpose in furthering the plot. Nor are these the least interesting characters; Mr. Micawber, Mrs. Gamp, Flora Finching, Mr. Crummles, Dickens' most brilliant figures, are given hardly anything to do; they are almost irrelevant to the action of the books in which they appear. (22–23)

Each year, the students are less patient with this objection, and I, as devil's advocate, must pull out all the variations that have been offered in the past 130 years to make certain that the class treats the question fairly. Doesn't Dickens' serial method of publication work like a soap opera, with each plot popping up in each number in a contrived way? Aren't there too many "kicks" arranged just to provide a thrill at the end of a number, with no internal logic?

And what about coincidences, some of which don't seem necessary even to advance one of the plots? No matter how much one appreciates the return of Micawber, can good sense accept his unexpected appearance before the Heep home in Canterbury in chapter 17 or his later appearance as Traddles' landlord? What mystic force draws Miss Murdstone into the Spenlow household just in time to meet David, puts Murdstone in Doctors' Commons just as David walks through, and brings Dr. Chillip into a particular inn just in time to meet David and complete the Murdstone story? Why should Ham, after saving any number of ships, finally give his all for the very ship that holds Steerforth, on a weekend when David comes to Yarmouth? What about the climactic grand reunions, not only in the antipodes but of Creakle, Littimer, and Heep in the model prison?

What about matters that cannot quite be called coincidences but still are unconvincingly convenient? If Dora's father stands in the way of David's marriage, kill him off; if Dora's usefulness to David is over, kill her off.

Finally, what about the changes in character that make plot events possible, while also making them highly improbable? If Heep must be defeated, Dickens turns Micawber into a character capable of prolonged and silent dedication to a complex task. If the Strongs must be reunited, Dickens provides Mr. Dick with the perception and tact of a first-class marriage counselor. Breaking my own rule about not leaving the text, I even bring in the background on the change in Miss Mowcher—a successful figure of grotesque menace converted into a sympathetic soul with a family, just because Mrs. Seymour Hill's feelings were hurt.

I reach for every objection I can find because the students themselves have, if anything, too little appreciation of conventional, "realistic" plotting. After all, this generation has been assigned *Mother Night, Catch-22,* and any number of other works in which theme controls plot events without disguise or hesitation. Their enthusiasm for all kinds of quest literature may also make them more tolerant of plot conventions than previous groups of students were. At any rate, they are almost too quick to dismiss improbabilities as unimportant.

In fact, I generally begin the rebuttal by focusing on those areas where the objection can be countered on the objectors' own grounds, those areas where Dickens is most concerned with probability and cause and effect. An easy first step for students is to find a handful of instances where Dickens uses the early chapters, the childhood chapters that everyone admires, to prepare for later events. Students are quick to come up with the repetition of the Clara story, the way Dora repeats Clara even to the words she uses. They are interested in how closely David echoes Murdstone and how Dickens makes certain we see the resemblance, even to having Betsey say, "Remember your own home, in that second marriage..." (ch. 44). They are also quick to delve into the precise details of Steerforth at school, the web of details that will make his exploitation of Emily, and the blindness of David and Mr. Peggotty, convincing.

We move to smaller matters—Emily's scene on the seashore and her early wish to be a lady, David's intimidation by the waiter in chapter 5 that will be repeated by another waiter, a coachman, and Mrs. Crupp. We might take up more subtle motifs, such as the wish for time to stop, that are echoed throughout the book.

I generally stop this approach just as it is getting interesting, leave the students to fill out more instances, and move on to the major rebuttal of the objection, which is of course that the fundamental coherence of the book is established not by some sort of statistical or "realistic" probability but by a theme that binds all together. Different critics emphasize different strands of the theme—Ford talks of the orphan as representing all humans in an unpredictable world (Introduction vii–ix), Q. D. Leavis points to the tie with the mother (47–64). I offer simply the larger term of "family." The class has already been introduced to the importance of domesticity as a Victorian value.

We can't examine all Dickens' variations on that theme in the time we have, but we make a few important lists. The first two have to do with the central theme of the book, David's struggles to find a family and found a family: first, a list of his parents and parent surrogates until he finds haven with Betsey Trotwood and, second, a list of steps in his progress toward the family that surrounds him at the end and has the right balance of love and security. (Some critics find this a progress toward the triumph of mindless, cold conventionality, but I leave that debate for another day.) I make sure that some of the quieter stages are appreciated, such as David's irrepressible habit of falling in love (Emily, Miss Shepherd, and Miss Larkins before he even meets Dora) and the care with which Dickens shows David's buckling down to work after Aunt Betsey brings him the news she is ruined.

Next we list all the other families in the book and ask whether they repeat (with variations, of course) or exactly reverse actions in the main plot. We list all the incompetent parents and debate whether even Peggotty and Aunt Betsey can be put in a "good parent" list. We examine how the Traddles plot is a simplified version of David's story and how the two families with obsessively possessive parents, the Steerforths and the Peggottys, destroy each other.

The interrelations proliferate until finally we bring up the Strong story, usually criticized as loosely connected to the rest of the book. We can demonstrate that it is tied to the other plots by multiple fibers: the bad parent reappearing in the Old Soldier, the family threatened like the Peggottys by a seducer and like the Wickfields by Uriah Heep, Annie valuing the balance of love and security that is the ideal in the book, and the "wise fool" Mr. Dick preserving this family as he had helped create David's second one.

At this point, Dickens may be saved from the accusation of carelessness, but he is in danger of being called excessively schematic. Finding patterns, as some recent studies have shown, not only can get to be a game but can falsify the experience of the book. Suppose the Strongs do fit like a piece of a jigsaw puzzle—do they work as characters? It's time to go on to another objection. First, however, I have to answer the student in the back row who insists that any connections we are finding are accidents. Without insisting that Dickens makes conscious decisions at every point, I use the occasion to recommend Butt and Tillotson's *Dickens at Work* and other sources of information on Dickens' planning and revising.

The next objection relates not to the plot but to the main character. I might quote from G. K. Chesterton:

> [*David Copperfield*] constantly disappoints the critical and intelligent reader. The reason is that Dickens began it under his sudden emotional impulse of telling the whole truth about himself and gradually allowed the whole truth to be more and more diluted. (*Charles Dickens* 130)

I might also cite A. O. J. Cockshut, "But if Dickens had a strong urge to speak publicly of his life and hard times, he also had an urge to falsify them" (116), or George Orwell, "David Copperfield (merely Dickens himself)" (51). David fails as a character because he is only a prettified version of his creator, a Dickens cleaned up for public view, with all of Charles's limitations, snobberies, and conventional prejudices and none of his charisma, genius, or revolutionary propensities.

I consider biographical criticism an absolute danger to undergraduate students because it seduces them into easy explanations, but one must be fair to this objection, so I grit my teeth and bring in every bit of biographical information that seems relevant: the Forster fragment, blacking factory and all; Maria Beadnell and all three Hogarth sisters; John Dickens' collection of novels and Charles's experience of Doctors' Commons; Charles's progress from shorthand reporter to writer of short pieces to novelist; his divided attitude toward his parents and his crusades for homes for fallen women and against the silent system in prisons. I point out that the book has odd changes in tone (such as when David sounds more like Charles criticizing Doctors' Commons in chapter 33), that Dickens encouraged the biographical connection and that *Copperfield* was his favorite book.

I do not encourage looking to all the events in the book that did not happen to young Charles. Instead, I put the students to a more difficult task that sends them directly to the text: Is David a character in his own right? Does he have a personality? Or is he only a puppet in a fake autobiography?

A majority of the class is immediately on David's side; they have already responded to him as an independent personality, whose continuity impresses even the psychology students. Here is a child who begins life in an Eden few children have ever known, who loses that Eden suddenly and violently but never loses faith that he can find it again: an enclosed world of love and security where he will be the adored center. Swiftly introduced to violence and cruelty of all kinds, threatened with that Victorian terror of falling through the middle class into the hopeless poverty and ignorance below, he discovers in himself considerable endurance, enough to survive the nightmare journey to Dover. Students find the young adult convincing as the child of that child: a little soft but capable of dogged persistence; always gullible, especially when around anything that reminds him of Eden; fond of things quiet and dreamy; generous but not perceptive of others' needs, especially when they conflict with his own; capable of accepting any amount of sacrifice from women as his right; and firmly holding onto the class and sex prejudices that have provided protection.

Students tend to be easier than critics are on the later David, partly because they are closer to his age and share more of his needs but mostly, I think, because they appreciate a hero with some flaws—the heroine has so few. They are willing to look in later scenes for complications that make him interesting, such as the mixture of his emotions when he finds Betsey is ruined (ch. 35). His persistent blindness—at the end of the book he's still convinced Steerforth had the seeds of greatness—students find more interesting for them than damaging to him.

They are also not much impressed with the argument that David doesn't really sound like a novelist, although they agree he is not likely to be a great novelist. Here we may indulge in pure speculation and imagine the books that David did write for publication: uplifting, pleasant, popular though of course never as popular as Dickens', moral without being demanding, always in the best possible taste.

Once we have seen both sides of this issue, an obvious next step would be to take up the question of sentimentality and melodrama in Dickens' style. However, I've never had much success working with this topic in my mildly dialectical style. The terms are too slippery and are used too carelessly by too many critics; we end up arguing terms instead of evidence. Thus I reserve this question for the examination of the novel's style that ends our discussion.

I do try to take up two more objections, always too briefly—that the women characters in *Copperfield* are poorly drawn and that the book is too cheerful. The woman question will wake up the weariest class; I don't need to provide a critical quotation, because the class is ready with its own pro and con examples. My job is to keep the focus on Agnes, Emily, Rosa, and Dora as characters in a book and then to clarify the different issues that the reactions present.

Immediately, we are into the fruitful question of the role of conventions in literature, both literary conventions and the ones literature borrows from society. By this stage of the course, students have been introduced to nineteenth-century stereotypes of women and have met them in other authors. They recognize the patterns into which the major figures of *Copperfield* fit. The issue becomes, does Dickens give any unexpected dimensions to the stereotypes, or does he use them as simply as some critics have suggested?

Interestingly enough, students often want to argue that Agnes is more than the stereotypical domestic goddess in that she is a believable and even sympathetic character, given the prison imposed upon her from her babyhood. If she lacks energy, she has admirable stubbornness; if she is very, very good, what advantage would there be in being bad? This line of inquiry can be helpful until its subject becomes a character Dickens should have developed rather than the character he did create. An always useful approach is to deepen the convention of the domestic goddess by presenting the relevant parts of Welsh's *The City of Dickens*. I then ask, if we see Agnes as expressing some of the most profound needs of Victorian culture, does the character mean more for the present-day reader?

I try the same method with Dora, presenting her as the embodiment of the comic principle or the essence of first love, but students find her all too real and totally unappealing. Rosa is a more rewarding subject, especially if we agree to ignore her speech over the prostrate Emily. We find both Rosa and Emily developing more dimensions as we investigate key scenes, and the question of whether they are effective characters begins to depend on the rhetoric that surrounds them. Therefore they too are pushed into the discussion of style.

My last objection—that the book is entirely too cheerful—produces no discussion at all. The class agrees that the ending is happy, that the book overall is cheerful, and that they want it exactly this way. After all the twentieth-century novels they've read, they find a cheerful book refreshing.

I don't try to argue them out of their pleasure. I do take the chance, though, to muse a bit on images that give the book an extra poignancy. The firelight at the Rookery, after all, is only a few yards from the graveyard. The snug little boat at Yarmouth is, from the beginning, menaced by the sea. In the haven of the last chapters, David remembers the ragged child who walked to Dover, and even in the recreated Eden, the sainted Agnes tells her children tales of witches. All through the book, David has tried to stop time and be safe from evil, but evil is always close by and time cannot be stopped. If Dickens gave up the subtitle, "Of the World as It Rolled," it was only because he had woven melancholy mutability into the texture of the novel itself.

Dickens' Problem Child

Thomas M. Leitch

Everyone knows that *David Copperfield* is the author's favorite child, but its favored status makes it, for critics and teachers, something of a problem child. Its peculiarly privileged yet denatured status in the popular mind—the position it shares with *A Tale of Two Cities* and *Great Expectations* as high-school Dickens, its unique standing as the Authorized Version of Dickens' autobiography—makes it harder to approach the novel critically, neither reducing it to an exercise in sentimental didacticism nor pigeonholing it as the exemplary Dickens novel. George Orwell and George H. Ford (Introduction) have written of the difficulty in responding thoughtfully to such a universally popular childhood book. How can a teacher deal with students' early memories of Peggotty and Uriah Heep, of David on the road to Dover and the shipwreck in Yarmouth, without dismissing them out of hand or accepting their invitation to read the novel as a series of picture postcards? How can the child's-eye view of *David Copperfield* be incorporated into a more comprehensive response to the novel, one that does justice to both child and adult as readers?

This pedagogical problem is closely linked to a critical problem. The place of *Copperfield* in Dickens' career has always been obscure. In a sense an autobiographical novel would seem the logical outcome of the "crescendo of restlessness" Edgar Johnson discerns in Dickens' life during the 1840s (*Tragedy and Triumph* 447) and the "massive return of the past" Steven Marcus finds in this period (283). The immediate product of these years, however, was not *Copperfield* but *Dombey and Son*; compared to such an ambitious and thematically programmatic novel, *Copperfield* seems formally regressive. If Dickens had never written the novel, his career from *Dombey and Son* through *Bleak House* and *Hard Times* would be marked by a growing interest in English society as such and a growing ability to use particular social institutions—the house of Dombey, Chancery court, Coketown—to represent the whole society. What place does the childhood idyll of *Copperfield* have in its immediate context and in Dickens' career as a whole?

Edmund Wilson's famous essay shows how clearly these two problems are related. Despite disagreements over details in Wilson's argument or over the psychoanalytic emphasis of his account, no one has seriously disputed Wilson's two major premises: that Dickens' career has an intelligible order within which each of his major works has its appropriate place and that his characteristic line of development is from the outside in. Thus, having early mastered the melodramatic, sentimental, discursive, and histrionic materials of fiction, Dickens only gradually discovered their potential for thematic significance. Wilson's leading argument—that "the work of Dickens' whole career was an attempt to digest [his] early shocks and hardships, to explain them to himself, to justify himself in relation to them, to give an intelligible and tolerable picture of a world in which such things could occur" (8–9)—should make *Copperfield* the pivotal work of Dickens' career. But just as *Copperfield* remains to the popular view a children's book, Dickens' idealized autobiography, or the quintessential Dickens, Wilson dismisses it as "a departure from the series of his social novels.... It is something in the nature of a holiday" (36–37). To accept this assessment is to admit the defeat of critical analysis, or rather to retire before analyzing. How can we honor *Copperfield*'s special place among Dickens' works while integrating it into his larger career? These problems arise most clearly and acutely in courses on Dickens (where *Copperfield* cannot be used simply as "the Dickens novel"), but they are implicitly present whenever *Copperfield* is taught.

Although a teacher lecturing on Dickens has roughly the same responsibilities as a critic publishing an article on him, a teacher leading a seminar or discussion group needs less urgently to give a coherent reading of any given novel. Indeed, a single coherent reading might well inhibit rather than encourage students' response to the work. In this sense, what are problems for the critic become opportunities for the teacher, whose primary aim is to provoke rather than to resolve discussion. This is particularly true of novels like *Copperfield*, whose comparative transparency makes exegesis unnecessary. Teachers make such novels more compelling not by making them seem simpler but by pointing out their complexities.

At the same time, the teacher must realize that much criticism does not work in the classroom. When Sylvère Monod writes that the opening chapters of *Copperfield* are the most successful part of the book because "they are so full of simple, fresh, direct observations that no reader can fail to find in the child David some part of himself," his observation is unexceptionable (313). But a teacher who made the same observation in class might provoke some such comment as, "Well, I didn't feel that way at all," or (more likely), "Yes, I did feel that way, but why?" If a single analytical reading of the novel can inhibit discussion, appreciative criticism cannot always do justice to Dickens' technical legerdemain or reveal the place of *Copperfield* in his career. The author of *Copperfield* is both magician and craftsman: the teacher's primary tasks are to demonstrate the nature and sources of the novel's uniquely enchanting appeal and to indicate its significance in the full context of Dickens' life and work.

When a novelist's discourse is as compelling as Dickens' in the opening chapters of *Copperfield*, a promising topic for discussion in the first class is the experience of reading, the way it feels to read the beginning of the novel. In describing the truthfulness of Dickens' rendering of childhood experience, Orwell concludes that he "has been able to stand both inside and outside the child's mind, in such a way that the same scene can be wild burlesque or sinister reality, according to the age at which one reads it" (17). Orwell might have observed further that to a reflective adult reader the child's and adult's perspectives in *Copperfield* are not alternately but simultaneously present, because of the irony that allows David to wonder, for example, as he first contemplates the Yarmouth landscape, "if the world were really so round as my geography book said, how any part of it came to be so flat. But I reflected that Yarmouth might be situated at one of the poles; which would account for it" (ch. 3). What Dickens captures here, through David's categorical judgment and preposterously illogical explanation, is not so much a particular landscape (though he does that too) as a quality of David's reaction—grave, absolute, unsentimental—to the landscape; the ironic adult perspective exposes David's perspective as limited and childlike without undermining its sense of matter-of-fact wonder. The balance Dickens strikes between the two perspectives becomes obvious mainly when he disturbs it in order to give the adult perspective priority, as in David's dark hints about Em'ly.

David's greatest and most enduring value to Dickens is precisely in the way he sees. Most of Browne's illustrations to the novel present him inconspicuously, as a spectator; often they show only his back; and with few exceptions, the center of interest in each picture is what he is watching, not himself. Although David is not simply a blank page or a witness to a parade of characters more interesting than he, *Copperfield* is not autobiography of the same sort as Joyce's *Portrait*: Dickens is not primarily concerned with the growth of his surrogate's consciousness.

David's double perspective begins as a specifically discursive or rhetorical device, a way of endowing otherwise unremarkable episodes with theatrical vitality by presenting them in purely external terms and deferring the explanation that would make them complete, demystified, and so uninteresting. Dickens' mystery plots are one expression of his love for withholding explanations, but even in a nonmystery story like *Copperfield* he engages his audience by implying deferred explanations. After Aunt Betsey returns from her drive with a mysterious man who has accosted her, David has occasion to look into her purse and finds that "all the guineas were gone, and only the loose silver remained" (ch. 23). The man, David eventually learns, is her former husband. Dickens might have established his existence in any of a dozen ways—for example, by way of explaining Miss Betsey's strange unwillingness in chapter 1 to accept her new niece as a boy—but by dropping unexplained hints, Dickens generates the greatest scenic interest in the earlier episodes.

Teaching a novel whose effect depends so largely on a double perspective raises two tactical problems. It is easy to indicate the presence and function of an adult perspective that constantly integrates experience into a retrospective pattern, for analytical criticism is inherently integrative. But how can one describe the childhood perspective, which places less emphasis on the analysis of experience than on the uniqueness of each person or event, except in the most general or impressionistic terms? And if one treats the double perspective of *Copperfield* as a specifically rhetorical device, what can one fairly make of its thematic implications—the pathos, for example, of David's faithful but uncritical presentation of his mother's self-dramatizing response to Murdstone's threatening courtship? Are such thematic implications rooted in a rhetorical technique, or do they serve as its basis?

Serious as these problems may be in teaching the discursive mode of *Copperfield,* they are easier to deal with fairly in class discussion than in a lecture or essay. However impressionistic students' accounts of David's childhood perspective may be, students are likely to value that perspective at least as fully and fairly as a publishing critic does if they are encouraged to use and compare their own childhood memories in assessing David's. And the debate over whether discursive or thematic motifs are primary and constitutive in *Copperfield*—whether (to take an extreme formulation) Dickens, searching for a way to justify his inveterate habits of mystification and theatrical prolepsis, had hit on autobiography as a discursive mode that would legitimate in thematic terms the double vision his rhetoric already implied—is ideally suited to open discussion. The double perspective of *Copperfield* is as likely to get evenhanded treatment in a seminar as anyplace else.

The opening chapters of *Copperfield* present a tour de force Dickens never repeated, and readers have often asked why not. As long as the analysis remains thematic, this question is impossible to answer, but if the opening chapters are considered as a technical experiment in double perspective, the answer becomes clear. For Dickens did repeat the experiment on different terms in *Bleak House,* where the alternation between the omniscient, ironic third-person narrative and Esther's ingenuous first-person narrative provides another kind of double perspective and where Esther herself, writing seven years after the events she recounts, attempts to give at once a sense of their immediacy and of their ultimate significance. After *Bleak House* Dickens seems to have decided that revelatory plots provided deeper thematic resonance to his double perspectives than did retrospective first-person narratives: he returned to a first-person account in *Great Expectations* only to complicate and undermine it by such ironic revelations.

As Pip's narrative progresses, his perception of a pattern shaping his life becomes more openly and trenchantly ironic, but from the viewpoint of discursive irony, David's growing up is simply a regrettable necessity, because his mature view of life is not interesting enough to make up for the charm Dickens loses when he closes the gap between David the narrator and David the involved observer. When Miss Murdstone, unexpectedly returning to David's life, is introduced as Dora's "companion and protector,"

Dickens writes: "A passing thought occurred to me that Miss Murdstone, like the pocket instrument called a life-preserver, was not so much designed for purposes of protection as of assault" (ch. 26). The distance between the two Davids has been effectively closed by now. The reflection is no less amusing for being within David's compass at the time he is supposed to have made it, but it is less expressive of his particular state of awareness; it is simply a good Dickens remark that does nothing to engage the reader further with the character who makes it. To compensate for this loss of discursive engagement—the older David's narrative being less interesting than his earlier narrative—Dickens offers another kind of engagement. Just as Charlie Chaplin, having begun a film with enough gags to make the audience laugh, might continue to develop the sympathies he had engaged through emotional modulations, Dickens, having first used David's views of characters like Em'ly, Traddles, and Mr. Mell to engage the reader's interest, counts on the reader's curiosity about their fates and desire to have virtue rewarded and vice avenged to maintain interest and broaden its thematic implications. The principal character for whose development Dickens solicits imaginative sympathy is of course David, the education of whose "undisciplined heart" (ch. 45) provides the novel's organizing theme.

It is impossible to teach *Copperfield* without discussing the thematic evolution of David's heart to the point at which it can balance affection and judgment. The development of this theme through David's life and the lives of analogous minor characters and the care with which Dickens has planned incidents and revelations to make this development clear have often been discussed, most fully and perceptively by Gwendolyn B. Needham. But such studies, which inevitably focus on Mrs. Strong's speech to her husband in chapter 45 as the thematic center of *Copperfield*, seem strangely irrelevant to the novel's greatest strengths; they seem more appropriate to the novel Dickens may have wished to write than to the one he actually wrote. John Butt and Kathleen Tillotson have shown in great detail how deliberately Dickens planned the pace and variety of the monthly numbers of *Copperfield* and the development of the novel as a whole (114–76); in some ways it is the most carefully plotted of all Dickens' novels. But this plotting is in general mechanical or superficial; for, to borrow R. P. Blackmur's distinction between executive form and the classic or theoretic form that underlies it, the plot of *Copperfield* is "nearly only executive form" (271). Dickens' adroitness in managing his large cast of characters, alternating comic and pathetic subplots, and pacing the revelations that provide David's education is impressive, but it is the same kind of skill that goes into a well-constructed detective story, and by itself it would not make *Copperfield* memorable. David grows up mainly by looking and learning, by applying the lessons of his acquaintances' lives to his own, instead of by his progressive or evolving interaction with them.

Because Dickens had not yet realized, as he would so brilliantly in *Bleak House*, the metaphorical implications of plotting (construction and revelation) for readers who might learn more than his characters, *Copperfield* has in a fundamental sense no plot at all, only a series of moral lessons, the most important of which come out of David's marriage to Dora. Although the lessons have an integral—as it were a pedagogical—structure, the novel in which they appear does not.

Again this critical problem has a pedagogical dimension. If Dickens, in the later chapters of *Copperfield*, loses the unique advantages of David's double perspective on people and events without gaining the corresponding thematic density, structural cohesion, or revelatory momentum that a more closely integrated plot would provide, what can be said in later classes on the novel? Once the interest in David's childhood perspective has run out, how can *Copperfield* be taught? In general, the obvious way to teach a novel this long is first to focus on its discursive aspects, which even students who have read only the opening chapters can appreciate, and later to emphasize the thematic and structural aspects revealed by the design of the novel as it unfolds; and *Copperfield* seems to encourage this progression. But thematic approaches to the novel, although they provide ample material for discussion, tend to reduce it to a tiresomely self-congratulatory tract on how to learn virtue from the misfortunes of one's friends. One can resist the temptations of such coherent but misleading interpretations by recognizing that the momentum of *Copperfield* is provided by teleological implications that, oddly enough, are not really a function of the plot: we read on because we want to see what is to become of David and all the others. Dickens deliberately plays with these implications in many ways: in his portentous early hints about the fates of Em'ly and Steerforth, in Micawber's repeated proclamations that catastrophe has come on him, and in David's initial reaction on meeting Dora: "All was over in a moment. I had fulfilled my destiny. I was a captive and a slave. I loved Dora Spenlow to distraction!" (ch. 26). *Copperfield* occupies a crucial position in Dickens' career for at least two reasons: it is, together with *Dombey and Son*, the work in which he first rejects the structural conventions of picaresque and melodrama and conceives of his principals in terms of a teleology of action; and the hero whose teleology Dickens explores is here an autobiographical figure, so that the novel examines by implication the teleology of its author's life. But this examination is best approached indirectly, by discussing the development of minor characters like Micawber.

Broadly speaking, fictional characters may be divided into purely histrionic conceptions and figures who in their very conception imply a teleology. Dickens' early novels offer an unrivaled panoply of characters conceived histrionically, so many, in fact—Mr. Pickwick, Alfred Jingle, Sam Weller, the Artful Dodger, Mrs. Nickleby, Vincent Crummles, Dick Swiveller,

Sally Brass, Sim Tappertit, Pecksniff, and Mrs. Gamp being only the most obvious—that it is difficult to recall histrionically conceived characters in English fiction outside Dickens. By the end of his career, however, such characters become fewer, more perfunctory, and less important than characters conceived in terms of teleological development, like Pip, Eugene Wrayburn, and Bradley Headstone.

In this respect *Copperfield* is clearly a pivotal work. Dickens' experience with Walter Gay (*Dombey and Son*), whom, relenting, he saved from the ignominious failure originally planned for him, and Miss Mowcher, whose character he softened in response to complaints from her original, seems to have taught him that even the most strikingly histrionic characters have the capacity for development. Grotesques like Micawber and Mrs. Gummidge seem complete when Dickens first presents them, but Dickens discovers in them the possibility of an unexpected but convincing turn, a transformation or apotheosis, that supplies them with a retrospective teleology. What is more logical than that Mrs. Gummidge, who seemed destined to wear out her days as a "lone lorn creetur," should offer strength and consolation to Mr. Peggotty in the face of disaster? What is more satisfying than that the warmly impecunious Micawber should (however implausibly) unmask the more systematic swindler Heep? What is more likely than that Heep himself should end his career as a model prisoner? In presenting grotesques who allow the possibility of a single unexpected reversal or apotheosis—one-trick ponies, as it were—Dickens is moving toward the creation of characters conceived in teleological terms.

Of all the characters in *Copperfield*, the one who most frequently and self-consciously defines his life in teleological terms is Micawber, whose every letter to David presents his misfortunes as if with final retrospective authority. His first letter concludes with the announcement that

> this is the last communication . . . you will ever receive
>
> From
>
> The
>
> Beggared Outcast,
>
> WILKINS MICAWBER (ch. 17)

Every letter announces with equal assurance that Micawber's life has run its course until Micawber, arrested again for debt on the eve of his departure for Australia, writes from prison, "The fair land of promise lately looming on the horizon is again enveloped in impenetrable mists, and for ever withdrawn from the eyes of a drifting wretch whose Doom is sealed!" only to add in a postscript, "I re-open this to say that our common friend, Mr. Thomas Traddles (who has not yet left us, and is looking extremely well), has paid the debt and costs, in the noble name of Miss Trotwood; and that myself and family are at the height of earthly bliss" (ch. 54). Micawber's mercurial responses to his immediate circumstances, his insistence at every moment that the pattern of his life is now complete, mock and trivialize the very concept of teleology. The extravagant ebullience and despair to which he is subject serve as a warning that a given life may resist definition from any particular vantage point, that in fact his resistance to teleological determination may be precisely what defines him as a character.

However inconsequential Micawber's gusts of emotion may seem, it is important to recall the teleological impulse he embodies. Although John Forster quotes numerous references Dickens makes to his father's letters as the basis for his character's gorgeous rhetoric, Micawber's tendency to see irreversible doom in every financial setback is evidently an expansion of a particular incident: John Dickens' announcement to his twelve-year-old son, as he was taken off to the Marshalsea, that the sun had set upon him forever (1: 16). Like Micawber, the elder Dickens was wrong; he was out again in a few months. It would be a typical and logical use of autobiography if Dickens, reflecting on that pronouncement over many years, had explored its teleological implications by making it more consequential, either by making Micawber's prediction come true or by showing that, metaphorically, it was already true (he does something of this sort with William Dorrit, who is broken by the Marshalsea and destroyed by the prison of the larger world). But with Micawber Dickens seems to do exactly the opposite. Micawber's dire predictions never come true, and since he is David's friend rather than his father, David is doubly protected from their consequences. It is as if Dickens wished, in dramatizing this traumatic episode from his past, to display it in suspended animation, apart from any consequences it might have for himself or for his hero.

The autobiographical impulse in *Copperfield,* speaking more generally, is an impulse to externalize the events of Dickens' early life, not only making them public and fictional, but also distinguishing, after the opening chapters, between their moral value as direct influences on the hero and their gnomic and histrionic value as dramatic spectacle. This is why, once the Murdstones and the blacking house are left behind, David's claims on us are so much less compelling: Dickens has given him adventures that remain largely external to him. David learns about life by observing such figures as Micawber, but he has no more direct interaction with them than he might have with a series of allegorical paintings in a museum: nothing Micawber does ever threatens him personally. (When the elder Dickens, by contrast, told his son, newly installed in the blacking factory, that the sun had set on him forever, the boy felt as if "they had broken my heart" [Forster 1: 16].) Even reversals that seem to endanger David directly—his aunt's loss of her money, for instance, or Spenlow's opposition to his engagement—seldom disrupt his life seriously or for long. The exception in the later chapters of the novel is David's romance with Dora, which emerges for this reason as the most successful aspect of these chapters, transcending Dickens' incessant attempts to turn Dora into another lesson in life.

To the degree that autobiographical works are designed to vindicate or reassure the author, the point of *Copperfield* is clear: one may achieve success by conceiving life as a spectacle or series of tableaux; one can learn and grow and know oneself (as David finally recognizes his love for Agnes) by observing other people. Dickens must soon have realized the limitations of this rather narcissistic wisdom, for he took pains to make his next observing consciousness, Esther Summerson, as morally responsible as any character in fiction, and he devised for *Bleak House* a plot that, in bringing together Jo and Lady Dedlock, dramatized the responsibility of every member of society for every other. When Dickens returns to the first-person mode in *Great Expectations*, his point is similar, for Pip also comes to full knowledge of himself through knowing other people; but since he learns that figures like Estella and Magwitch can never be external to him, he pays more dearly for his knowledge than David ever does. Pip is no mere observer.

But just as a lecture or article that emphasized the thematic coherence of David's education would mistake the true sources of the novel's power, an assessment of *Copperfield* as an unfinished sketch for *Great Expectations* would seriously underestimate that power. Again, class discussion has the advantage of exploring Dickens' thematic structure without presenting it as the last word on the novel: David may take Mrs. Strong's effusion as an authoritative comment and influence on his own development, but for Dickens' readers it is more properly a subject for debate. Perhaps the most judicious way to summarize David's relation to his education is to point out that although Steerforth's treachery and Heep's scheming—unlike Murdstone's cold cruelty—do not threaten him directly, he feels the pain they inflict on his best-loved friends, the Peggottys and the Wickfields, as extensions of his emotional sympathy. In other words, Dickens uses autobiography as a mode of social awareness, a way of generalizing issues of personal power and morality to a vision of society as a network of moral responsibility. The importance of the novel lies finally in David's gradual and incomplete evolution from a purely discursive function, a way of seeing and talking, into a morally responsible agent, a person who feels and acts through social relations. In the later novels Dickens employs a double perspective to emphasize the atomistic individuality of each character and his or her commonality with all other characters through the social order; in *Copperfield*, the double perspective focuses more often on experience itself, on the uniqueness of each moment and the ultimate meaning it incarnates. Because this double perspective is indispensable to understanding the position *David Copperfield* enjoys in the minds of author and readers alike, it provides the strongest line to take with Dickens' problem child.

David Copperfield in a Children's Literature Course

Beverly Lyon Clark

"Let me suggest several reasons why you may not want to take this course," I say to the eighty or so students who have materialized for the first meeting of "Children's Literature." They include first-through fourth-year students, some of them prospective teachers; most are majoring in something other than English. "For one thing, this is not exactly the small discussion class you may have hoped it would be. For another, the final exam is on the last day of exams, in the afternoon. Finally, look at the syllabus. This is not an easy reading course. Our first book, *David Copperfield,* is 950 pages long. True, we'll be spending two weeks on it, but that's still a fair amount of reading to get through in two weeks. . . ."

These comments hint at my impure motive for teaching *David Copperfield* in "Children's Literature": to winnow out the serious from the hordes who seek an easy way to fulfill a distribution requirement. But I have purer reasons as well. Dickens' novel, unlike most recent fiction, addresses all ages: both children and adults can delight in its evocation of childhood. Moreover, *David Copperfield* is often considered suitable for adolescents, and I include adolescents' as well as children's literature in the course. The trend in the book's readership resembles that of fairy tales: initially told to an audience of all ages, they are now considered children's literature—though I doubt that *David Copperfield* will ever descend (or ascend) to the exclusive realm of the nursery.

In addition to being children's literature (in the broad sense), *David Copperfield* is about children's literature. It comments on children and literature—on what children are like, how they should be treated, and what they should read.

Dickens provides insight into what children are like through his sensitive portrait of David, who, like other children, is egocentric, literal-minded, impressionable. David thinks Peggotty must be handsome, for instance, because he likes her so much and because her coloring matches that of an attractive red velvet footstool. Or, when told that Miss Murdstone sleeps with one eye open, he concludes that she doesn't, for he tries it and discovers that it can't be done. And, when his mother dies, he grieves—yes—but he also derives satisfaction from being a cynosure for the other boys.

Dickens likewise dramatizes conflicting nineteenth-century attitudes toward children, both directly and metaphorically. Peggotty and the Murdstones, for instance, take opposite approaches—both present in Victorian England—to child rearing. Peggotty's loving care is congruent with the Rousseauian and romantic belief in the child's natural goodness, the Murdstones' harshness with the Calvinist insistence on original sin.

Dickens himself prefers Peggotty's approach and seems to believe in the child's innocence, sensitivity, and susceptibility to feeling and imagination.

Peter Coveney argues that for Dickens, as for other nineteenth-century writers, the child became a symbol for feeling and imagination in opposition to encroaching materialism. Thus the child should be nurtured, not tortured. Yet, as Angus Wilson suggests, Dickens' tortured, isolated, and neglected children, like David, are often strangely nurtured by this treatment:

> for all that [Dickens] cries out (and with utter sincerity) against the abominable distortion that such isolation, neglect, or faulty teaching brings, it is exactly these cut-off children (even those like Lou Gradgrind who have been deprived of the healing springs of childish legend and fancy) who "wonder", who gaze into the fire and dream dreams, that are worth more than all the Christmas laughter and glee of the ordinary children whom Dickens exhorts his adult readers to care for. (205)

In Dickens' own life, "although [his] genius might have been utterly lost through the neglect and incomprehension of his parents, it was in fact fed and developed by the half-knowledge of an ugly world that he gained by this very neglect" (207). Dickens may thus be a little ambivalent about the best treatment for children.

In the latter part of the book, after David has grown up, Dickens continues to portray nineteenth-century attitudes toward children, but metaphorically rather than directly. Much as some of the children have been like adults (witness Agnes), many of the adults are childlike, even childish. Mr. Dick, for instance, is literal-minded: when told that his new accommodations don't provide room to swing a cat, he earnestly insists that he doesn't want to swing a cat anyway. These child-adults become touchstones for the other characters: anyone who respects Mr. Dick can't be all bad. Yet child-adults often cannot handle responsibility. Thus Dora's incompetence as a housewife becomes a touchstone, testing David's patience and love, and the choice of such an unsuitable wife reveals David's own immaturity and irresponsibility. Dickens' metaphoric child-adults hint at the range of Victorian attitudes toward children—and perhaps at the conflicts in Dickens' own mind.

Dickens likewise reveals his opinion on another important issue of childhood: should children be permitted to read or hear fairy tales? He clearly disagrees with those who, like Gradgrind, would proscribe fairy tales, fearing that they encourage a child's fancy to run amok. For David, as for Dickens, fairy tales can keep the fancy alive in harsh circumstances and provide a modicum of comfort. Thus David frequently refers to stories like *The Arabian Nights* and *Robinson Crusoe*, which enabled him to survive his childhood. Nevertheless, such fantasies have their dangers, for they intimate not only the joys but also the dangers of enchantment—the seductiveness of Steerforth, the insidiousness of Heep. And living solely in a fantasy world, as David does when courting Dora, suggests too much distance from reality. Once again, Dickens' attitude takes on complex shadings, as he comments on children and literature in his literature for children. For he intimates that children need fairy tales, but not fairy tales alone. They need to balance fairy tales and reality.

David eventually achieves this balance (though angelic Agnes may be more of a fairy tale than he wants to admit), and Dickens himself integrates the two elements in his novel. Dickens interweaves fairy-tale plotting with a realistic social context, as Harry Stone has noted in *Dickens and the Invisible World*. Such a blending of fantasy and reality, such a heightening of reality, is common in much children's literature. *The Secret Garden*, for example, draws on a rich garden symbolism, for all its realistic surface, and *Alice's Adventures in Wonderland* sends a rather prosaic emissary from the "real" world into Wonderland. In *David Copperfield*, Australia is a kind of Never-never-land where castoffs can succeed, and, as Stone points out, Betsey Trotwood is a kind of fairy godmother (197).

I attempt to cover all this material and more in three eighty-minute class meetings. But I don't just lecture to students: I want them to acquire more than a Gradgrindian collection of facts; I want them to learn to think, analyze, synthesize. Thus I rely on that oldest of pedagogical tools—the question. When broaching the issue of Dickens' portrayal of children, for example, I ask students whether they can think of instances when David exemplifies—to use Piaget's terminology, introduced on the first day of class—egocentrism, literal-mindedness, transductive reasoning. Then we can go on to assess how perceptive Dickens' portrait is. Even in a class of seventy or eighty, so large that only a few individuals speak, asking questions can still encourage each student to think.

Furthermore, I give students individual or group assignments in class. I ask individuals and then small groups to rate the following couples, ranking from the good marriages to the bad: Clara and David Copperfield, Senior; Clara and Mr. Murdstone; Peggotty and Barkis; Dr. Strong and Annie; Betsey and her husband; David and Dora; David and Agnes. (Ranking exercises seem unusually effective in generating small-group discussion, because they require students to make a commitment.) The large-group discussion can then encompass such issues as appearance versus reality (whom does Annie really love?) and Dickens' methods of characterization.

Another exercise that I tried this past year was effective, though I need to work on it more. I started discussion one day by announcing that the class had been invited to Fantasy Island, where each student would encounter two characters from *David Copperfield*, characters with whom she could have adventures, develop relationships, whatever. Each student had to choose two characters. I then announced that the trips had been rescheduled because of heavy demand and that students had to travel in groups of five or six; each small group had to agree on which characters they would encounter. Some chose sweetly good characters like Agnes. Others were attracted to Steerforth. One group wanted to meet the Murdstones—to subject them to unspeakable tortures. Once the students had discussed the characters, the class as a whole could discuss what the characters are like: whether they are multidimensional, whether they change, what their relations with others are. At least, that's what I could have done and what I hope to do this year. The exercise certainly seemed successful in engaging the students, but I need to work on channeling that engagement into our discussion of the characters.

In any case, the exercises and questions get students actively involved in learning, not just passively receptive. (Where did I see that people remember only twenty percent of what they hear but seventy percent of what they say?) I also try to engage students not just cognitively but affectively. I suppose that such an approach is appropriate in a course on children's literature, for a child's response to literature depends heavily on feelings and attitudes. But even college-age students learn better—and more eagerly—when affectively engaged. Part of what we should teach in literature courses is the power of language, "the shock of recognition that the encounter with it brings about," so that teaching is "a kind of oscillation, a playing back and forth between the experiential and the intellectual in which the first continually gives way to the second and the second is then refreshed by the first" (Borroff 15).

How successful is my inclusion of *David Copperfield* in "Children's Literature"? Certainly the students have not been altogether convinced of its value in the course. On final evaluations they respond with more catcalls than cheers. But the usual complaint is the book's length—not a telling objection (and, after all, I invite it the first day of class). My favorite is the comment, "Too long, boring and out of touch with today." (It would be easy just to laugh off the remark or to wrinkle up my nose in disgust, but I suppose she was telling me I didn't engage her interest, didn't make the book relevant enough.) Another student has asked, "Is *David Copperfield* primarily a children's book? I didn't read it until eighth grade." (She makes me wonder when she read *The Hobbit,* another course text—but in any case she apparently missed my statement that we would be reading both children's and adolescents' literature and that *David Copperfield* is not only for but also about children.) Still, there are some who find *David Copperfield* "very beneficial" or who "particularly enjoyed *David Copperfield* because it was a book that appealed to all ages."

Despite the mixed reviews I'll continue to teach *David Copperfield* in "Children's Literature." For one thing, I think my opening gambit works—I think that students are more serious about the course when I open with

David Copperfield than they were before. It sets the tone for the course. Moreover, the book dramatizes nineteenth-century attitudes toward children and the characteristics of children: it not only is children's literature but is about children and literature. And of course *David Copperfield* is a splendid novel with which to start examining the techniques of literature and their impact—on both children and adults.

An Introduction to Fiction:
David Copperfield in the Genre Course

Margaret Scanlan

For the past several years, I have regularly taught at Indiana University at South Bend a sophomore-level course called "Introduction to Fiction" in which *David Copperfield* plays a prominent part. This experience has made me aware of how congenial genre courses are to the more extreme formalisms, of the extent to which they embody the view that literary history, as Edward Said puts it, consists of "fraudulent genealogies entirely made up of books stripped of their history and force" (25). This purblindness—which Ellen Cantarow compares to the notion that the earth is supported by an endless chain of elephants, "all the way down, nothing but elephants" (66)—menaces all genre courses, but the teacher of fiction faces special difficulties. All too often, in my experience, we encourage the idea that the development of novelistic technique from Dickens to Joyce or Woolf can only be applauded. This view of the novel progressing from gig lamps to luminous halos, from baggy monster to significant, economical form, inevitably obscures much that is rich and vital in the traditional novel; oddly, it also obscures its modern elements, its "technical achievements." While I am still willing to concede that the genre course can teach students to read closely, give them an awareness of the formal elements in fiction, and provide a useful critical vocabulary they can carry into advanced courses, I am also concerned that they continue to respond to the moral and political issues that it raises and that formalist criticism denigrates. In teaching *David Copperfield*, then, I emphasize the complex characterization of the hero, Dickens' sophisticated sense of time, and his use of myths and archetypes—all features often considered the property of Proust or Joyce; at the same time I hope to convey enthusiasm for his vision of the social world, for the lively exchange between literature and life that the novel promotes.

One pleasure of teaching *David Copperfield*, as opposed to, say, *The Wings of the Dove*, is that students actually like Dickens spontaneously and do not regard their instructor's pleasure in the text as professional affectation or mental aberration. In a general way, I think one should see the job as trying to increase the number of elements in the text to which they can respond without being too quick to find sophisticated objections, even in the face of such affronts to the jaded sensibility as Mr. Peggotty's "treasure in heaven" speech or Agnes generally. Therefore I am willing, after the first lecture on Dickens' life and a talk on autobiographical transformation—avoiding simplistic identifications, seeing how writers assimilate their lives to a fiction, how a fiction is a way of coping with one's life—simply to play the good audience. I think one should encourage, by reading out loud or simply by picking up on students' responses to questions about characterization, a sense of the emotional range in the novel: it is moving, it is funny. Nonetheless, because a college sophomore already has some preconceptions about traditional novels, Victorians, and popular writers, it seems important, that first day, to plunge into the text's difficulties and insist that a good reading complicates our perception of the text, alerting us to its nuances rather than systematizing it.

To this end, I introduce the problematic hero, pondering at some length the first sentence and its numerous implications. It is only fair to admit that, like many other teachers, I have been induced to see the benefits of analyzing the first sentence not only by the undoubted critical benefits but by the knowledge that my students are unlikely to have read far the first day. My plan to spend five seventy-five-minute class periods, or two and a half weeks, on *David Copperfield* reflects a similar realism about how much students at a commuter campus are able or willing to read for one class. I explain why, in an ideal world, everyone would have read the whole novel before we begin to discuss it, but I do not attempt to force that issue, instead asking people to divide the number of pages by five and read accordingly. I come to class with a set of questions that are meant to elicit certain kinds of responses, lead the class in certain directions, though few have "correct answers." Of course, responses are not always the ones I had in mind, and the direction—and certainly the depth—of discussion will vary accordingly. It is occasionally a liability to have the only script for the classroom drama, and I always have to work at suppressing the urge either to prompt the students or play their parts myself. Thus when I ask students to react to the first sentence, I cannot be sure that they will say everything I had in mind or that I will not have to break into a short lecture if a crucial point goes begging. What follows, then, is a modestly platonic model of a discussion of *David Copperfield*—some issues and questions that I have found helpful, with an indication (more historical than fictional, but still a composite) of the response that my students have made and that I think others would be likely to make.

As we talk about the first sentence we comment on how much less vivid David seems than many other characters in the novel, on the possibility that he may behave unheroically or badly, on the self-consciousness of writing a novel that will somehow evaluate his life. I note that unlike *Jane Eyre*, which we have just finished, this novel contains many references to the act of writing it and that the feat of memory entailed will be a consistent theme. While to Jane the past and its pain are always immediate, David will recognize, especially in the beginning, that memory selects and may idealize. I ask the students to identify passages from the first chapter that show different points of view about the past—the child's view, the adult's view, hearsay, and combinations of these. The idea, of course, is to encourage students to see that they must read for multiple points of view even though the novel has only one narrator, to note that David's opinion at one juncture may not be his final one. Jane never misjudged anyone's character; David so often does that we must keep that possibility in mind to the end.

Two passages seem to warrant introduction on the first day even though most of the students haven't yet reached them. The first is David's characterization of the novel as "my written memory" in chapter 48. Those sensitive to language will pick up the difference between "written memory" and some locution like "an account of what I remember." While "psychological realism" is an issue to be developed later, I point out that the actions of the novel often seem not only to be remembered but to imitate the actions of the memory, as when Miss Murdstone keeps popping up like an ill-repressed childhood injury. The second such passage, much discussed by the critics (see especially Gilmour and Lankford), is the evocation of Canterbury Cathedral:

> The rooks were sailing about the cathedral towers; and the towers themselves, overlooking many a long unaltered mile of the rich country and its pleasant streams, were cutting the bright morning air, as if there were no such thing as change on earth. Yet the bells, when they sounded, told me sorrowfully of change in everything; told me of their own age, and my pretty Dora's youth; and of the many, never old, who had lived and loved and died, while the reverberations of the bells had hummed through the rusty Armor of the Black Prince hanging up within, and, motes upon the deep of Time, had lost themselves in air as circles do in water. (ch. 52)

To analyze this passage fully requires, of course, an essay in itself: in teaching I emphasize its beauty and underscore the notions that the novel's presentation of time has an almost Proustian (not the adjective for the classroom) complexity; that we are seldom allowed to remain firmly anchored in the present, as we were in the first novel of the course, *Emma*; and that this way of seeing time, even this language about time, appears again in many modern novels.

Although I do not encourage the students to carp about Dickens, at some point early on, after we have already discussed the discontinuities and complexities in David's identity, after we have begun to look at the role of memory, someone is sure to object to the text's improbabilities, to the lack of realism in what the student believes to be a realistic novel. In real life, the reversals in David's fortunes after his trip to Dover would never occur; the Micawbers would not reappear in so many disconcerting places, especially not as Traddles' landlords; Betsey's husband would not be buried on the thirty-sixth anniversary of their wedding; and so forth. I encourage people to add to the list. What is the real objection? That life, at least as it is lived in South Bend, Indiana, in the late twentieth century, does not offer so many vindications or coincidences. (Frequently there is a latter-day Julia Mills in the class who can put this truth poignantly.) Should realism mean "what would be likely to happen to me"? Scenting a trap, at least one sophisticate will say no, sometimes embarking us on a course of historical relativism. Yet when one examines the list of coincidences and improbabilities, only Dora's timely death really seems easier to explain in a nineteenth-century context, and then only if one ignores Jip's death. History will not get us out of this one, so we must look elsewhere; fortunately, the first day's look at David and memory disinclines students to the view that Dickens was simply pandering to a popular audience or was too slow to know what he was doing. How, as a New New Critic might say, can we "recuperate" the text? If such coincidences and vindications are not part of our day-to-day experiences, where do they take place?

At this juncture several hands are usually in the air, with people quick to point to dreams, legends, and fairy tales—or, if I am really unlucky, to soap operas and trashy novels. Apparently, then, our unconscious minds tell us stories that deeply correspond both to the oldest stories our culture tells us (look at all the vindicated orphans in mythology and the Bible) and to the most popular art forms. The measure of Dickens need not, then, be our own sense of probability: his novel is not only or even primarily "realistic," in a naive sense, but it has a dimension of psychological realism, even perhaps of myth.

At this point my own reading draws heavily on essays by Shirley Grob and Christopher Mulvey, but especially on Harry Stone's *Dickens and the Invisible World*, as I encourage students to think of parallels between events and characters in the novel and those in fairy tales: Betsey as bad/good fairy, David's fear that Peggotty will lose him, wondering if he could be found by her buttons, the goroo man, and so forth. What effect do these "fairy tale" elements have on the story? Students give various responses but generally agree that we are conditioned to expect a happy ending, that characters like Betsey and Mr. Murdstone seem larger than life because they have so many resonances for us, and that the story becomes "mythic"—that is, not only the history of David Copperfield but the immemorial adventure of growing up—in part because of the fairy tales. The last two points, at least, make the Dickens text seem complicated and rich rather than merely improbable.

Many of my students are quick to identify the Christian elements—losing all that one has, the famous "baptism"—in David's flight to Dover and his renaming, but they need to see that the text does not, all the same, encourage simplistic identifications of the hero with Christ, à la *Grapes of Wrath*. I also ask students to talk about places in the text that refer to dreams or have the quality of dreams. Again, listing or free-associating soon presents a number of examples: the tempest, the frustrations of David's first trip to Salem House, the dream after David meets Steerforth at *Julius Caesar* (the literary allusion can be linked to the Bible and fairy tales), David's insomniac visions of Uriah sleeping on his couch. We then discuss the common elements in these disturbing dreams and their significance, especially as they foreshadow (or in the tempest embody) unacceptable knowledge. While I usually defer a full-scale discussion of the tempest to the last day, I at least plant the suggestion here that the drowning of Ham and Steerforth, which to the common-sense waking mind seems the most melodramatic coincidence in the novel, is the sort of association that happens all the time in dreams.

David's obsession with these two characters opens the whole issue of his "guilt" with respect to Yarmouth. Surely there is something equally suspect in the preoccupation with Uriah Heep that turns the latter's visit to David's rooms into a kind of nightmare? What do David and Uriah have in common, anyway? Following Stone again, we note the common qualities of these fatherless boys who aspire to the law and Agnes' hand. My students do not know the story of Uriah and Bathsheba, so I tell it briefly. No one is willing to argue that Dickens could have chanced on such an odd name as Uriah, and at this point people accept the principle that older stories play an important role in *David Copperfield.*

Talking about myths and dreams in this way liberates the class from a narrow notion of realism and a patronizing view of Dickens as melodramatist. It makes a novel easily read for entertainment richer, more complicated, more suggestive. Since we talk about the human needs to which the fairy tales and Bible stories respond, the issue of literary allusion gets introduced without the suggestion that it is a pretentious, self-contained game. Joyce, Kafka, and Faulkner, whom we read later on, are less of a shock to students who have seen that even a traditional novel is partly organized by myths and not only foreshadows but actually contains elements of psychological realism.

The discussion on the third and fourth days develops the issue of David's complexity and the theme of memory, as we discuss his relationship with Steerforth, his marriage to Dora, and the tempest scene. We also talk about the novel's many subplots and the minor characters they introduce, first as they relate to David and then to the entire book. Here Norren Ferris' discussion of Micawber's teaching David about language and Stanley Tick's essay on the relation between Mr. Dick's Memorial and David's novel seem especially helpful. Then I ask the students to think more generally about what subplots do for a novel, reminding them of how isolated the heroes of many characteristic novels seem to be. Students usually note the role subplots play in sustaining suspense, their "color" and interest, as well as the notion of the minor character as an alter ego for the hero and his or her fate as an alternative for the hero. But I am especially interested here in stressing the point about the "dense social world" of the traditional novel that Iris Murdoch makes so effectively in "Against Dryness": the novel's vivid realization of so many people from several social classes prevents the fantasy that other people are only a projection of the hero. They have a life the hero cannot control, and they too are affected by money and politics and other forces that originate outside the psyche. For Murdoch, this sort of realism is morally valuable; I try to persuade students to consider her view carefully.

At this point I raise the issue of social commentary in novels by introducing Virginia Woolf's famous objection to those Georgian novelists who seem to ask the reader to "write a cheque" ("Mr. Bennett and Mrs. Brown" 105). Should the novel be conceived as a self-contained world, as Flaubert, Joyce, and Woolf believed? Or was Sartre right in arguing (in "What Is Writing?") that the referentiality of language makes every novel an action, not an aesthetic object like a painting or a musical composition? Where does Dickens urge us to take action, to confront the reality behind his fiction? Is it a flaw that he does so? I am not after a class concensus on this point, but I want the students to see that social argument is not limited to graceless works like *The Jungle* and can coexist with stylistic interest and complicated narrative perspective. I also want them to see some distinctions in the text itself: most agree with the critics that the penitentiary scene is too loosely connected to the narrative to be really effective but find the more integral child-labor theme moving. Does sentimentality hamper social statement? I point to Mr. Peggotty, perhaps reading the offending speech about the mothers of France. The more sophisticated, thinking they can identify the cue, laugh; others, however, argue that the goal of social reform justifies sentimental appeals to a mass audience. This argument is close enough to G. K. Chesterton's to warrant describing his view of Dickens as "reforming optimist." According to Chesterton, Dickens was more successful in promoting social reform than were writers of a more naturalistic bent (e.g., Hardy, Gissing, Gorky), whose stress on the misery of poverty inadvertently dehumanized the poor: "All the despair about the poor, and the cold and repugnant pity for them, has been largely due to the vague sense that they have literally relapsed into the state of the lower animals" (*Charles Dickens* 197). While many college sophomores have not read the "reforming pessimists" Chesterton cites, they are likely to have read *Native Son* and can see the interest of Chesterton's argument in the contrast between Dickens' poor people and Wright's.

The charge of sentimentality comes up again in our discussion of the happy ending. In earlier weeks, with Frank Kermode's *The Sense of an Ending* in mind, I have already discussed the conventional happy ending and tried to undermine students' faith in the happy endings of *Emma* and *Jane Eyre*, or at least to show the problems. Students are primed to look for difficulties, and most locate them in David's prolific but unpassionate marriage to Agnes and in Emily's horrible exile. We talk about the audience's expectation of a tidy ending and note that this one seems almost like a parody, with even Mr. Mell dusted off and rehabilitated. If we have trouble believing in this resolution, why? There is, of course, no right answer, but students who have begun to see the novel's complexity sense that Dickens seems to have written a book too problematic for this aspect of his form.

From *David Copperfield* we go to *Madame Bovary, The Metamorphosis,* and *Dubliners,* accompanied by Flaubert's and Joyce's polemics against the traditional novel. I want students to enjoy these novels while remaining aware that their authors' critical views tend to disguise their relation to what has gone before. Without tendentious discussion of influence, I think students who have looked at the nightmarish Mr. Murdstone and his black dog can see Kafka as extraordinary but not unprecedented, can see a line of descent from Micawber's tyranny over words to Joyce's puns. I think, too, that they realize why happy endings disappeared or understand the modernist's fascination with a mental world. But I also hope they have a sense that something was lost when the novelist ceased to turn the reader, again and again, to the world that produced them both, when he or she lost confidence in the novel's ability to change—and not just provide an alternative to—that other world outside its boundaries.

The Chords of Memory: Teaching *David Copperfield* in the Context of World Literature

Willis Konick

> If our affections be tried, our affections
> are our consolation and comfort; and
> memory, however sad, is the best and
> purest link between this world and a
> better.
>
> *Nicholas Nickleby* (ch. 6)

Teaching world literary classics to undergraduates becomes, in my experience, a matter of text selection and adherence to some underlying theme. For teachers of world literature face the danger of creating an intolerable variety. Since we constantly work with texts not clearly joined by country, genre, or period, we must substitute our own sense of harmony for the congruity a single nation or author would naturally introduce. We must decide which common point of view, stylistic mode, or choice of character, scene, or plot will join together our disparate texts. We must seek, as we select our texts, some strongly felt consistency and hope our students sense that consistency as well.

Therefore, when approaching Charles Dickens as a source of texts for courses in world literature, I ask myself which Dickens novel I prefer, and consider what particular harmony that Dickens novel promotes, what other novels or short fiction or even drama might join my selection and produce a digestible whole. I also find that in such instances I start with Dickens and then add the rest: he is so great, so seminal, so familiar to our culture that texts following his must bend to the principal theme or attitude his novels offer. At this point the problem of selection grows more complex. I must ask myself not only which Dickens novel but which Dickens I prefer: the merry Dickens, the satiric Dickens, the sentimental Dickens, the Dickens who encapsulates Victorian England, the Dickens who favors criminals or children, the Dickens who wonderfully conceives "flat" characters (to use E. M. Forster's well-known distinction), unchanging and therefore memorable types. For Dickens is not Kafka, though the resemblances are striking. Those themes or attitudes that the works of Kafka suggest, for teachers of world literature, are captured by that splendid adjective "Kafkaesque." "Dickensian" is a more inchoate term.

My first impulse, when constructing a course on the foundation of Charles Dickens, was to rely on Dickens as master of types, as purveyor of major figures who naturally call to mind the notion of the grotesque, from monstrous Quilp to equally monstrous Miss Havisham. Once I had made this choice I could easily establish a harmony. This Dickens guided me inexorably to the major works of Nikolai Gogol: *The Overcoat, The Nose,* and *The Diary of a Madman; Dead Souls,* Gogol's only novel; and his great comic drama *The Inspector General.* There one discovers those same extravagant, unchanging figures one found in Dickens. Akaky Akakievich, curious hero of *The Overcoat,* the clerk of clerks, whose genesis, station, and profession have made him (until the misfortune of the stolen overcoat) a contented copying machine; Chichikov, the hero of *Dead Souls,* a conniving gentleman who expertly resists each provocation to plunge below the surface of life; the gallery of landowners in *Dead Souls,* types conceived broadly in order to encompass instances beyond the bully or miser or sentimental gentleman; and the ingeniously corrupt town officials of *The Inspector General.* It is not difficult to combine these major Gogol works with *Martin Chuzzlewit, Bleak House,* or *Great Expectations* and suggest a deformed and therefore accurate vision of deformed humans at their labors. And it is not difficult, with Dickens and Gogol behind one, to move on to Kafka, Joseph Heller's *Catch-22,* and Vladimir Nabokov's *Lolita.*

David Copperfield might also take part in such a harmony, though less successfully. Certainly the array of unchanging types in *Copperfield* equals those in other Dickens novels: the Micawbers and Uriah Heep, Mr. and Miss Murdstone. But *David Copperfield* as a novel of recollection, as Dickens' initial first-person narrative, suggests another harmony that demands emphasis not on grotesque vision but on the world and substance of one's childhood. Or at least that was the consistency I felt, in selecting *David Copperfield* as the foundation for a course devoted to world literary classics. Therefore I joined *Copperfield* to novels in which the force of memory, particularly childhood memory, predominated. The texts I chose to supplement *David Copperfield* were Fyodor Dostoevsky's *The Adolescent,* Yukio Mishima's *The Temple of the Golden Pavilion,* and Louis-Ferdinand Céline's *Death on the Installment Plan.* I would like to comment here on Dickens' relation to Dostoevsky and Céline; Mishima offers equal potential but would carry us beyond the focus of this short essay.

My starting point, in selecting *David Copperfield,* was that David does not wish to claim distinction, even narrative distinction, that he describes not the force of a single personality but the force of memory itself. Even memory does not remain the sole property of the hero; he easily apportions memory to members of his family and to his friends of youth. His special attribute lies in that greater force which memory conceives, that phenomenon which suggests a mingling of souls. David's remembrances ("I picture") always draw into his field of vision other people, other places: beloved Peggotty and her Yarmouth home appear; characters whom David has not yet met emerge, most notably Steerforth, who figures largely in David's thoughts even before he arrives at Salem House. David's process of recollection arouses, either really or potentially, the powers of observation, the remembrances, of other characters: the job of recollection becomes communal. In other well-known first-person narratives—Tolstoy's *Childhood*, for example, or Charlotte Brontë's *Jane Eyre*—one must imagine the narrator as a photographer, who gazes at the ground glass and then, as the appropriate moment arrives, closes the shutter to catch the fleeting expression of his subject. In such works the narrator's mode of observation dominates. In Dickens' case one must imagine that the photographer graciously invites those who have gathered round him to inspect the ground glass as well. Even the subjects may abandon chair and floodlights to examine the spot they once occupied. Later, photographers of the Dickens sort will set a self-timing device so that they, their assembled friends, and their subjects, may all gather before the camera to be photographed. If *David Copperfield*, as first-person narrative, functions as a springboard for the examination of other such narratives, David must be compared to narrators who acknowledge that perception, even memory, is a kind of public trust, to narrators who do not push their memories far without consulting their compatriots.

Our first indication that memory will prove communal arrives in the novel's opening pages. The hero is born posthumously—his father dies some six months before his birth—yet his memories of his father's gravestone, of the "indefinable compassion" that stone aroused, are among the first remembrances he wishes to report. The reputation of the dead man sparks his consciousness. The late father, whose name David bears, brings to the novel Betsey Trotwood, another absent figure of formidable reputation, who appears and disappears during the first hours of David's infancy. He brings David's mother to the novel; since she is much younger than he, he must have actively pursued her. He also bears responsibility for the appearance of our narrator; David seems a much desired child. The dead father who lives in recollection inspires more than warm and compassionate remembrance, however. He inspires that impulse to share the narrative which so defines his son, for he demonstrates, as posthumous father, that the major happenings of our lives are linked by unseen hands, unseen encounters, which, though unobserved, prove the mutuality of all phenomena.

We must now add the other parent: Clara Copperfield, a precious figure, recalled in almost reverential detail. Yet she attains her greatest influence on David and is most strikingly represented when she stands ready to depart from the novel, to become herself a memory. David returns home from school and finds his mother nursing an infant son: a second child revives those images of mother love the senior child has long retained. The

mother clasps son to son and, swayed by implicit passion, she offers her
breast to both: she draws David's head to her bosom, so that he may nestle
there with his new brother. The force she now attains and the artistic
motive for inserting the child (who dies soon after) most fully emerge as
David takes his final leave from his mother. In a striking moment of the
novel, the mother holds up the new child to David, as if to stamp on his
memory the significance of infant consciousness, as if to conjure up an
emblem of the child in us all:

> I was in the carrier's cart when I heard her calling to me. I looked out,
> and she stood at the garden-gate alone, holding her baby up in her
> arms for me to see. It was still cold weather; and not a hair of her head,
> not a fold of her dress, was stirred, as she looked intently at me,
> holding up her child.
>   So I lost her. So I saw her afterwards, in my sleep at school—a silent
> presence near my bed—looking at me with the same intent face—
> holding up her baby in her arms. (ch. 8)

The salutary force of the mother's consciousness, the memory of *her*
memory, becomes even more decisive as David flees the hated confines of
Murdstone and Grinby and the wrongful indigence he has suffered. A
single recollection guides David to Dover and to Aunt Betsey's home.
Though the aunt wrathfully abandoned Clara and David when the newborn
child turned out not to be the favored girl, and though she has made no
effort to rediscover David since his infancy, David's mother has recounted
many times the moment when the dreadful Betsey disclosed an ounce of
compassion among her pounds of rage: she abruptly touched the young
mother's hair. That moment of natural tenderness treasured by the mother
is, at her death, passed on to David's storehouse of vivid recollection, to be
doubly cherished there, as treasured family artifacts acquire double value
among the members of a new generation.

> But under this difficulty, as under all other difficulties of my journey,
> I seemed to be sustained and led on by my fanciful picture of my
> mother in her youth, before I came into the world. It always kept me
> company. It was there, among the hops, when I lay down to sleep; it
> was with me on my waking in the morning; it went before me all day.
> (ch. 13)

David is thus guided by a "picture," as he calls it, a picture that has long
dwelt just below the threshold of his consciousness, based on the feeblest of
evidence (a hand touching hair) and fostered by his mother's stories of Aunt
Betsey. When David, unaided, must escape the intolerable command of

Mr. Murdstone, a picture rises to the surface of his consciousness and suggests the direction his flight must take. Memory here sustains the organism; the life of one or several beings may be balanced on this slender rope, pulled taut by circumstance and made strong by hope.

Others are also guided by memory. Emily, in her flight from Steerforth, arrives at restoration of full memory when the child calls her "fisherman's daughter" and fashions the arch that joins the present to the past. Though Steerforth appears to have little recollection of his childhood, others remember for him. Rosa Dartle bears the scar of his childhood rage; David bears the memory of those stories he once narrated at Salem House, waiting for Steerforth to drift into sleep. A full adult life is confirmed by some force that springs from childhood years, underscoring the mutuality of human experience. If one swerves too sharply from that childhood truth about oneself, one makes a bad or even self-destructive choice—for instance, David's choice of Dora, who revives his mother's role as child bride but fails to suggest that deeper seriousness his mother once conveyed by holding up the new child as token to her departing son. If one bears little memory of childhood or spends one's childhood acquiring the art of adult crime, like Uriah Heep, one's chances of becoming a villain in the Dickens mold are good. Without the force of childhood memory, one loses humanity and never feels a natural union to the souls of others. The individual becomes distinctive in the worst sense and thus grows isolated from others.

Departures from the path suggested by childhood memory are difficult to correct: the proper road soon drops from view and returns only as the vision of a vision. The road now grows distant from one's present neighborhood but returns in sharp particularity when one recalls the curve where a childhood cycling accident took place or the sign that marked the merging of city into countryside. When David reflects on his faulty choice of marriage partner, when he imagines what his marriage might have been had he found union with a woman as steadfast and adoring as memories of Clara Copperfield and Clara Peggotty, a vision of Agnes arrives.

> When I thought of the airy dreams of youth that are incapable of realization, I thought of the better state preceding manhood that I had outgrown; and then the contented days with Agnes, in the dear old house, arose before me, like spectres of the dead, that might have some renewal in another world, but never more could be reanimated here. (ch. 48)

Nor will David find the serenity that right choice generates until, after Dora's death, he asks Agnes to become his wife. Only then do chords of memory, like some celestial instrument, accompany his choice. For Agnes, like David, is another natural reservoir of recollection:

> With her own sweet tranquillity, she calmed my agitation; led me
> back to the time of our parting; spoke to me of Emily, whom she had
> visited, in secret, many times; spoke to me tenderly of Dora's grave.
> With the unerring instinct of her noble heart, she touched the chords
> of my memory so softly and harmoniously, that not one jarred within
> me; I could listen to the sorrowful, distant music, and desire to shrink
> from nothing it awoke. (ch. 60)

Readers of *David Copperfield* generally agree that Agnes, the temple of
rest and peace, is a kind of cipher in the novel. But David's attraction to
Agnes is striking and psychologically true. It derives from the stirring of
memory beyond memory, the conjuring up of feelings so subterranean
they cannot be listened to directly but may be heard only as an echo,
reflecting back from cavern walls.

In the final pages of *The Brothers Karamazov*, Alyosha Karamazov, one
of the novel's triumvirate of heroes, speaks to the boys who surround him
regarding the force of childhood memory. They have assembled both to
mourn and to celebrate the death of Ilyusha Snegiryov, the boy who sought
to retrieve his father's honor (a singularly unselfish action in a novel whose
prime subject matter is parricide). Alyosha and his young friends gather at
the very spot where Ilyusha and his father often talked, thereby commem-
orating their filial union with a more deliberate, self-conscious mingling of
souls. Such mingling is expertly guided by Alyosha and expertly underscored
by Dostoevsky. Alyosha tells the boys:

> You must know there is nothing higher and stronger than some good
> memory, especially a memory of childhood, of home. People talk to
> you a great deal about your education, but some good, sacred memory,
> preserved from childhood, is perhaps the best education. If a man
> carries many such memories with him into life, he is safe to the end of
> his days, and if one has only one good memory left in one's heart, even
> that may sometimes be the means of saving us. (epilogue, ch. 3)

As Clara Copperfield once held up her new son like a banner to be
contemplated by her departing son, so Alyosha Karamazov asks these boys
to contemplate the emblematic nature of Ilyusha's death: it is a memory
they cannot and must not lose, for it is a memory shared. And in Dostoevsky, shared memory, so significant to Dickens, acquires still greater
primacy and becomes, in Alyosha's terms, good memory, a force that
might unify all humans, that might create a golden age, when souls no
longer mingle but combine. Alyosha here insists such good memories point
their bearer toward positive action, because, as the entire novel affirms,

they invite us to compassion, while bad memories, or the absence of childhood memory altogether, lead us to cruelty, indifference, or despair. When Dmitri Karamazov moves toward rebirth, when he grows ready for his own terrifying journey, swaddling, and new selfhood (his own variant of David's journey to Aunt Betsey), when he is stripped naked by relentless interrogation, he dreams a curious dream. In the dream he sights a babe, a suffering child, whom he now wishes to rescue, thus rescuing all who weep and shiver, half-clothed, unfed: "Tell me why it is those poor mothers stand there? Why are people poor? Why is the babe poor? Why is the steppe barren? Why don't they hug each other and kiss? Why don't they sing songs of joy? Why are they so dark from black misery? Why don't they feed the babe?" (bk. 9, ch. 8). The innocent child of the dream suggests not only the pitiful, half-clothed Dmitri who now sleeps but the pitiful, half-clothed Dmitri who as a child ran about bedraggled and uncared for, another victim of his father's apathy. The adult Dmitri has despised the child Dmitri as he has despised his father—the neglected child and the neglectful father both speak to him of that great human failing, indifference to the pain of others. He seeks ineffectually to correct this failing by rescuing maidens in distress (Katerina Ivanovna), but he perpetuates it by contributing his share to human heedlessness: he callously humiliates Captain Snegiryov, the father of Ilyusha (and thus the father of the child who brings good memory to the boys). Only now, as childhood memory returns to him, can Dmitri pity the victimized child, pity all babes, and thereby pity himself, forgive the child he once was. But to pity oneself, though an essential first step, is not to share one's memory. Thus Dmitri moves from that single suffering child to a sense of suffering that might bind us all.

> And he felt that, though his questions were unreasonable and senseless, yet he wanted to ask just that, and he had to ask it just in that way. And he felt that a passion of pity, such as he had never known before, was rising in his heart, that he wanted to cry, that he wanted to do something for them all, so that the babe should weep no more, so that the dark-faced, dried-up mother should not weep, so that no one should shed tears again from that moment, and he wanted to do it at once, regardless of all obstacles, with all the recklessness of the Karamazovs. (bk. 9, ch. 8)

Though Dostoevsky employs childhood memory more rigorously than does Dickens, the function of shared memory is much the same: such remembrance nullifies adult cynicism and alienation and draws humans to the humane. Those double images so characteristic of *David Copperfield* recall our wondrous connection to the child in us: the young boy son stares at the baby son; the dead Steerforth calls forth the youthful, sleeping

Steerforth; the child who was once the fisherman's daughter regains identity when she comprehends her name anew; Agnes in the present is amplified by an Agnes who summons up agreeable domestic memories. Dostoevsky employs similarly double images in his own novel: Dmitri dreams of the suffering child he once was and the pitying child he has now become; Alyosha convinces his young comrades that the memory of Ilyusha Snegiryov exemplifies good childhood memory of any sort, that Ilyusha's image will return in later years.

Such parallels suggest a joining of Dickens and Dostoevsky, and their union has been frequently promoted (see Katarsky and Lary). Yet their common passion for crime and criminals, their love for melodrama and convoluted plots, and their attraction to the city and its more unfortunate inhabitants should not obscure all that separates them: Dostoevsky's greater frankness, less genial comedy, and more incisive religious thought; Dickens' greater gift for startling character and image and striking propensity for lengthy, governing metaphor. Only one factor joins them absolutely: their common judgment that shared childhood memory acts as antidote to human isolation.

A similar commingling of memories occurs in the only major Dostoevsky novel written in the first-person form, *The Adolescent* (or as it is sometimes translated, *A Raw Youth*). Arkady Dolgoruky, the novel's hero, not only acts as a David-like narrator but seeks to reconstruct his half-forgotten memories of his mother and father, reconstruct the childhood that illegitimacy, neglect, and his own resentment have obscured. Again the novel suggests double images everywhere; the child consistently shadows the adult. Arkady is himself half child, half adult; childlike in his naiveté and vivacity, adult in his skepticism and sharp, probing intellect. Early in the novel Arkady wanders down somber Petersburg streets and spots a child who has lost his way. Once more, as in *Copperfield* and *Karamazov*, the chasm that divides the self from its later years collapses; the lost and frightened boy is, in most respects, Arkady as we know him: newly arrived in Petersburg, sometimes bold, more often fearful, a wayward child himself.

> I saw a little boy, so little in fact that I was surprised he was alone in the street at such an hour. It looked as if he'd lost his way. A woman stopped next to him for a moment, but apparently she couldn't understand what he was saying because she shrugged helplessly and walked on, leaving the child alone in the darkness. I went over to him, but for some reason the sight of me frightened him and he rushed away. (pt. 2, ch. 4)

One last European novel suggests the force of memory and offers us another first-person narrator whose consciousness absorbs the point of view of others and then reproduces that consciousness as if it were his own.

Both David and Arkady are marvelously buoyant; hard labor at Murdstone and Grinby and illegitimacy do not defeat them. But Ferdinand, the narrator-hero of Louis-Ferdinand Céline's *Death on the Installment Plan*, is far more resourceful than they. He survives a childhood of excruciating sadness, of anxiety so hyperbolic that his disquiet grows intentionally comic. Running to and fro on the orders of his parents, young Ferdinand cannot even pause to defecate; he empties his bowels in flight, like (his own simile) a storm-tossed bird. As for his memories, their abundance threatens to overwhelm him. Ferdinand complains: "I was myself, a putrid smell" (306). Such words suggest that the memory-laden mood of Dickens and Dostoevsky has been revived, now in another urban setting—Paris before World War I. There Ferdinand, like Arkady and David before him, fabricates a pattern of images, drawn from the consciousnesses of others as well as his own, that constitutes his fund of memories. In this case the fund is devastating: a crazily indefatigable mother and a wrathful father; a series of unhinged employers; a lunatic teacher and a lunatic inventor; disagreeable neighbors and disloyal friends. And when this cast of characters is not sufficient, he introduces great fragments of the populace of Paris through the medium of superb hallucinatory scenes. They busily fill up Céline's overcrowded stage, to offer us the mingling of souls in new fashion. The flood of vigorous memory breaks its banks, and one-time neighbors, deceased kinsmen, lost comrades appear, washed up by a consciousness that cannot cease to recollect. Ferdinand thus celebrates a curious imbalance: each newly acquired memory subtracts from that store of moments available to us, for at life's terminus a door will close and our power to remember will then cease. Yet the power of memory also sustains and invigorates us; it gives full meaning to the moments that remain. In Dickens and Dostoevsky the character who remembers best lives the longer or more satisfying life. In Céline such a character best comprehends the force of death. Ferdinand does not prematurely leap toward death, and he struggles to resist as best he can. Yet his native realism causes him to embrace death and thereby to spend his life in mourning, in laying up memories. In doing so he apprehends the dualism that visits those who think on death. He grieves over death's consequence: a life of ceaseless loss. But as he grieves the fact of death is paradoxically revoked, for in memory the dead again arise and the confines of a single consciousness recede. That memory may well be shared proves just as meaningful for Céline as it does for Dickens and Dostoevsky.

At the end of *Death on the Installment Plan* a grieving Ferdinand returns to his Uncle Edouard, after the death of his inventor patron, Courtial des Perieres. The burden of memory now threatens to defeat him utterly. But Edouard swaddles him in new clothing:

"You can't run around in rags...I'll go get you a pair of pants...Wait a second...I'll find something..." He went to the next room and brought me a whole suit, out of his closet with the sliding door...in perfect condition...and a bearskin coat...big and shaggy..."You can wear these for the time being..." He also gave me a cap with flaps and a suit of flannel underwear...I was all set up.... (575)

Céline thus remembers David Copperfield, Mr. Dick, Aunt Betsey Trotwood, and the arrival at Dover. Rebirth is not too mighty a phenomenon for a novel that appears to direct itself unswervingly to death. Ferdinand is ready to strike out again, to refuse this kind uncle's offer of asylum, and to join the army. New memories await this memory-encumbered hero. New souls queue up to merge with his. Another history waits to be written, in the spirit of *David Copperfield*. For though Ferdinand, Arkady, and David ostensibly compose their own biographies, in truth they write the biographies of others. They become that medium by which memory thrives, that instrument by which memory sounds its distinguishing chords, both joyous and melancholy.

Fathers and Sons: *David Copperfield* in a Course on Victorian Autobiographical Prose

Gerhard Joseph

"An artist chooses even when he confesses," Valéry tells us, "perhaps above all when he confesses." The apothegm captures the spirit of a course I teach in Victorian prose, open to upper-division undergraduates and graduate students, that features *David Copperfield* as a central document. Because the context of the other books in the syllabus shapes the approach to Dickens, let me list the works in the largely historical order we read them: Erik Erikson's *Young Man Luther*, Thomas Carlyle's *Reminiscences* and *Sartor Resartus*, John Stuart Mill's *Autobiography*, Charles Dickens' *David Copperfield*, George Eliot's *The Mill on the Floss*, John Henry Newman's *Apologia pro Vita Sua*, George Meredith's *The Ordeal of Richard Feverel*, Edmund Gosse's *Father and Son*, Samuel Butler's *The Way of All Flesh*, and Franz Kafka's *Letter to His Father*. While I try to see each book "as in itself it really is," however naive that Arnoldian ideal may strike some these days, my choice of texts establishes a focus that moves from the generic to the thematic. Whatever skewing there is (and I shall admit below to certain simplifications) follows from that twin focus. My approach is loosely, eclectically psychoanalytic, combining the languages of classical oedipal theory, of Eriksonian ego psychology with its emphasis on "identity crisis," and (by final-examination time) of Lacanian definitions of the "signifier's" oedipal desire. As for *David Copperfield*, through a series of allusions to Chaucer, Shakespeare, Milton, Blake, Wordsworth, and Keats, I try to place the novel within the "Great Tradition" of English literature. And since my students are intensely urban, upwardly mobile, and vocation-oriented (my school, Lehman, is the senior college in the Bronx of the City University of New York), I stress the role of the city in David's progress.

Charting the convergence of nonfictional and fictional prose genres, we examine the kinds of self-revelation that nineteenth-century authors in a confessional mood apparently intend (stressing the theoretical problems accompanying the concept of intention) and the rather different impressions readers sometimes take away, partly for reasons of genre. The broadest aims are to distinguish autobiography from the autobiographical novel and to indicate at the same time how these forms invade each other's boundaries. Whatever innocence the student may bring to the distinction between fact and fiction in general and between the factual and fictional autobiography in particular is thus, one hopes, severely qualified by semester's end. To that purpose, discussions of supposedly nonfictional autobiographies (say, Mill's) accentuate the writer's imaginative selectivity, suppression of psychically dangerous material, artful control of point of view—that is, all those procedures we are apt to associate with the novel. Conversely, discussions of the fictions stress the ways in which their authors render certain biographical materials with painstaking—and frequently painful—verisimilitude. And even when the novelists transform details of their lives as we know them from other sources, such masking is all the more revealing because it tells us what the writer needs to suppress or highlight.

Thus, if we are looking for straightforward, undeflected revelation, *David Copperfield* contains details that are corroborated by such standard biographical authorities as John Forster and Edgar Johnson. Chapter 4, for instance, itemizes the books, mostly eighteenth-century novels, that the young Dickens read, and we can nowhere find a more compelling picture of the wretched months Dickens spent in Warren's blacking factory than the account in chapter 11. But, the transformations, the ways in which David's life diverges from that of Dickens, are finally more significant than such controls. The most important alteration is that David has lost his biological father before the novel's opening, while John Dickens was an all-too-palpable presence in his son's life. It is from this difference that the thematic reason for the novel's inclusion in the course arises. For what most of our confessional texts have in common is the treatment, either in passing or as a leading structural motif, of the Victorian father's power both to facilitate and to obstruct the son's maturation. (Perhaps a word is in order about the three texts that do not fit this mold precisely. To suggest the universality of the theme and of our loosely psychoanalytic approach to it, I provide an extra-Victorian frame, opening the course with *Young Man Luther*, the psychohistorical analysis of a son's life-and-death struggle with the father/Father in an earlier period, and ending it with the most chilling modernist statement of the theme, Kafka's *Letter to His Father*. And I include *The Mill on the Floss* to show that a young woman's struggle with Victorian patriarchy has its resemblances to but also its differences from a young man's—a motif exemplified in *David Copperfield* by Agnes Wickfield's problem with her father.)

Victorian patriarchy in its psychohistorical dimension is thus a second concern of the course, complementing generic discrimination as a background to *David Copperfield*. The final section of Lawrence Stone's *The Family, Sex and Marriage in England, 1500-1800*, a book I put on library reserve, provides ample documentation for the popularly accepted notion that the Victorian period, the heyday of the paterfamilias, witnessed a late flowering of unrestricted paternal authority among the middle classes. Certainly the family historian's generalization is substantiated by the continuing appearance of powerful fathers in the course. James Mill, James Carlyle, the Tulliver men, Sir Austen Feverel, Philip Gosse, and Theobald Pontifex are, to be sure, rendered with varying degrees of affection and respect; the father does not inevitably do irreparable damage to the son or daughter. But each of the fathers, for good and/or ill, is a towering presence to be grappled with.

In this light, *David Copperfield* is one of the two works we consider (Newman's *Apologia* being the other) that lacks a biological father with whom a protagonist must contend; indeed, it is precisely the obtrusive presence of the father in the other books that highlights his apparent absence in Dickens' novel. The biographical facts that the novel transforms make David's orphaned condition, in a book swarming with orphans, all the more revealing: John Dickens was a complex force in his son's youth, as the account of his early life that Dickens wrote out for John Forster (and that I outline for the class) suggests. The spoiled offspring of servants to an upper-class family, full of genteel illusions despite his position as an improvident clerk in the Navy Pay-Office, the elder Dickens was, in K.J. Fielding's apt characterization, "affectionate, hard-working, and generous, but so easy-going that he spent money and borrowed it with the same happy facility, and without a thought of the future. As a rich man he would have been an ideal father; on a salary of £200 to £350, he wore out the patience of both his friends and family" (2). His confinement to the Marshalsea debtor's prison during a particularly bad stretch of financial weather led to what most readers have seen as the most scarring event of the son's psychic development: his consignment to a dirty, rat-infested dockside warehouse for a four- to five-month period of labelling pots of blacking. The sense of utter desertion was only reinforced when John Dickens, though released from the Marshalsea after receiving a fair-sized legacy, failed to rescue a miserable son from *his* prison until a slight quarrel broke out between the father and the manager of the warehouse. The entire humiliating episode is of course adumbrated in Murdstone's banishment of David to the factory of Murdstone and Grinby.

Thus, if Dickens was not literally an orphan, the condition in which he found himself was pretty much that of David in the novel (and was the existential plight of several other Dickens heroes from *Oliver Twist* onward)—"a child of excellent abilities and with strong powers of observation, quick, eager, delicate, and soon hurt bodily and mentally" who is utterly "thrown away" at an early age (ch. 11). While Dickens blamed both parents for their callousness, he reserved a special ire for his mother. Not only had she been primarily responsible for getting her twelve-year-old son the position at Warren's—through the favor of the manager, a relative of hers—but once the father had finally procured the son's release, it was she who was intent on his return. "I do not write resentfully or angrily," said Dickens in his account of the matter for John Forster, "but I never afterwards forgot, I shall never forget, I never can forget, that my mother was warm for my being sent back" (1: 32). The very intensity of blame directed at the mother (and the novels are full of mothers insensitive to their children's woes) tended in part to exonerate the father. Such partial exculpation may at any rate explain the ambivalence Dickens shows toward the father in

David Copperfield by "splitting" him into various surrogates, just as he splits the son. My analysis of the novel itself consequently breaks, quite simply, into two parts as I ask the students to consider how first each of the individual "sons" and then each of the "fathers" contributes to a total filial configuration.

In discussing such psychic fragmentation, I relate it to the larger aesthetic impulse of what Steven Marcus has called Dickens' "analogical imagination":

> By multiplying a particular character or situation, and embodying within a single work manifold and significantly diversified images of the same kind of person or relationship, Dickens was able to render the conceptions in his novels more dramatic, subtle and complex than he could have done through any other resource compatible with his kind of genius. (40)

While Dickens shares this tendency with other expansive English writers, like Chaucer and Shakespeare, who strive to give us God's plenty, his fecundity of character differs from that of his great predecessors in that it serves a primarily urban need, capturing the multitudinousness of the modern city. J. Hillis Miller has defined the quality in speaking of "the proliferation within each [novel] of a great number of characters, each different from all the others, and each living imprisoned in his own milieu and in his own idiosyncratic way of looking at the world" (xv). The potentially solipsistic inhabitants of the modern city must turn themselves into artists, as Dickens and David do, in order to comprehend it; they must attempt to "transcend the limitations of any single point of view by presenting as many as possible of the limited persons, and of the new aspects which the city gets when seen through their eyes" (xvi).

Dickens thus explores the abundance of possibilities open to the youthful city dweller, "an orphan in the wide world" (ch. 9), by having David work through and absorb various models of the self—delusory and useful, false and true, demonic and angelic—as his emerging consciousness maneuvers among a series of child-parent and then romantic relationships. David himself is relatively passive—like Oliver Twist before and Pip after him—as he seeks to forge a solid identity while for the most part finding one imposed on him. The largest educational question *David Copperfield* poses (an issue of direct relevance to the New York students I teach) concerns the alternative appeals of aggressiveness and gentleness in the "fight with the world" (ch. 10) that the novel's young, but especially its urban young, must undertake. And one can locate David's major foils, the novel's other fatherless sons (Steerforth, Uriah Heep, Ham, and Tommy Traddles), along a continuum between these polar oppositions. On the evidence of *David Copperfield*, the two avenues open to the Dickens orphan wandering in a dark and alien city are an aggressive self-imposition on it and a temperamental or principled passivity that trusts to the workings of a benign Providence—and Dickens seems to champion the latter value. The complementary villainies of Steerforth and Heep suggest that he disapproved of characters who "ride on" roughshod over others, however their orphaned condition may explain a passionate or calculating self-assertiveness. Yet Dickens felt himself to be precisely such an orphan of the city, thrown away as he was, and he was certainly no stranger to ruthless urges. His career as novelist and editor exhibits frequently enough a vain, ambitious, manipulative devotee of power.

How, I ask, can we explain this discrepancy between the life and the moral implications of the tale? The answer I try to elicit is that the work is therapeutic and cautionary for the author as well as for the reader: precisely because Dickens was far from meek, he was prone to argue—at least on the surface of his work—the self-chastising thesis that the meek and suffering shall inherit the earth. And when characters like Steerforth and Heep drive a novel forward with a demonic energy that recalls Dickens' own, their usefulness for the author reminds us of the subversive sympathy that Blake in *The Marriage of Heaven and Hell* attributed to Milton in his creation of Satan. As an antidote to that appeal, Dickens favors an innocent malleability—the twistability of Oliver and the tabula rasa impressionability of Pip and David (copper being the most pliable of metals) as well as the comic passivity of subordinate exemplars. Tommy Traddles' unobtrusiveness and tractability ("soft as ever," Steerforth chides in chapter 29), for instance, permit him to embody the moral ideal that the novel presents as a countervalue to "firmness" as a means of meeting the abrasiveness of "this rough world" (ch. 1). Not that firmness is simply equatable with hard-hearted villainy: if it is the favorite creed on which the Murdstones, both brother and sister, love to expatiate ("another name," the mature David realizes, "for tyranny; and for a certain gloomy, arrogant, devil's humour that was in them both" [ch. 4]), it is also the quality that Betsey Trotwood tries to inculcate in David, "a strength of character that is not to be influenced, except on good reason, by anybody, or by anything" (ch. 9). *David Copperfield* is surely the Dickens novel most directly indebted to the English Romantics in its celebration of childhood innocence and, as Carl Dawson has recently argued, in a Wordsworthian insistence on sublime Nature's ability to restore David to psychic health after Dora's death (132–43). But the softness-firmness opposition evinces the Romantic filiation most relevant to my concern because it presents for David, the emerging artist, the alternative appeals of "negative capability" receptiveness and a self-imposition on the world that partakes of the "egotistical sublime." Whatever characterological "roundness" (in E.M. Forster's sense) or aesthetic maturity David has achieved by novel's end results from his having passed through and internalized the supplementary principles of soft and hard, of pliancy and assertiveness, exemplified by the "flat" alter egos that surround him. That is one meaning of the deaths of the supplementary models, gentle Ham and "ride on" Steerforth.

That such a balance is uneasy and less than ideal may be gathered from a comparable splitting of the paternal principle into Mr. Peggotty, Murdstone, and Micawber. It might well be argued that the various sons of the novel are derivative in that they enact in a second generation the opposing tendencies of soft and hard fathers. In the seaside world of Yarmouth, which supplies a pastoral release from the city, the novel strives for its most pronounced mythic resonances in the Noah-like Mr. Peggotty. An archetypal Father of Us All in whom contradictions are resolved, the bachelor has created a comic ark for the sheltering of the world's "lorn creeturs"—Ham (his idealized "son"), Emily, Mrs. Gummidge, and, in the early sections of the novel, David himself. The ark is of course no final protection for his "children" against this world's deluges, both natural and human-made, but Mr. Peggotty exists as a mythic exemplar against whom the novel's more fallible parents, especially Murdstone and Micawber, ask to be measured.

The Murdstone-Micawber axis probably derives from Dickens' mixed feelings about his father that I have sketched in above, and in that sense David's two most obvious surrogate fathers are what Steven Marcus has called "symbiotic characters," characters who are best understood in relation to each other. Murdstone, a hard rock for the beating of copper, is Dickens' most menacing portrait of the paternal tyrant, the murderous stepfather of myth and fairy tale who tries to crush the spirit of the competitive young. Precisely because David's biological father is dead, the infant can in the novel's opening section enjoy his comparably childlike mother in a delightful Eden. Into the garden of Innocence there steps the usurping ogre Murdstone with his wicked mix of sadism and sentence to introduce the oedipal struggle of Experience. (I intentionally echo the Blakean contraries since, in order to distinguish David's life before and after Murdstone's entrance, I discuss the analogous difference between "Infant Joy" from *Songs of Innocence*, in which no blocking father impedes the loving dialogue between mother and child, and "Infant Sorrow" from *Songs of Experience*, in which the oedipal struggle is sullenly joined.)

But as unattractive a figure as Murdstone undoubtedly is, David can understand in retrospect the qualities in him that are useful and even necessary to the unprotected young: the darkly handsome suitor seems genuinely fond of Clara Copperfield, as she is of him, and she is attracted to him precisely because of his sheltering patriarchal "firmness." Since he and his sister are the first characters in the novel to announce this quality as their creed (ch. 4), I align with Murdstone (simplifying for the sake of course emphasis) all subsequent characters who counsel a Victorian firmness or "duty"—the relatively positive versions of the qualities, like Betsey Trotwood and the Wickfields; their sinister counterparts, Creakle and Uriah Heep; and finally the David who comes to prize discipline at the expense of softer virtues. Duty in the novel is not merely a convenient euphemism for sadism, sexual perversity, impotence, or flaccidity, but, as James Kincaid has argued, many characters use it as such a cover (175). For this reason, the "disciplined heart" that David evolves in his maturity constitutes the most important issue over which rival interpretations of the novel meet. On one side, the majority of critics, taking a position most directly advanced by Gwendolyn B. Needham, see the development of emotional control in David—the toughening, as he so often puts it, of his "undisciplined heart"—as a value the novel celebrates unreservedly. On the other, Kincaid best represents readers who find such an emphasis excessive because it underestimates the comedy, the youthful spontaneity, and the imaginative joy that subvert the somber and sentimentalizing maturation theme. (After a full exposition of the matter, I ask the students to take sides.)

The novel's lighter set of values has as its leading exemplar David's other "father," Wilkins Micawber. As I place, with but a slight exaggeration, all the proponents of firmness, discipline, and duty in a purview first defined by the Murdstones, I consider (again, granting a measure of special pleading in the service of course emphasis) the softer, less worldly, more childlike qualities of Clara, Dora, Mr. Dick, and Tommy Traddles within a festive ethos most triumphantly expounded by the Micawbers. As Kincaid encapsulates the matter in a chapter that does eloquent justice to Micawber's comic values, "the real conflict in the novel is between [Murdstone's] 'control' and Micawber's wild self-indulgence, between cash-boxes and steaming punch" (171). Murdstone may not be David's Henry IV, but Micawber is surely his Falstaff. The improvidence, the ingenuity, the verbal pyrotechnics, the utter imperturbability in the face of one financial disaster after another—above all the expansive love for all his children, including David (which renders our inevitable association of him with W. C. Fields so ironic)—make Micawber the larger-than-life fount of the novel's comic energy. Moralistic readers may see in him an early version of *Bleak House*'s Harold Skimpole, merely an amusing but "cadging scoundrel," in George Orwell's words (105). And because he subverts David's serious task of soul making, Dickens must finally banish him as Shakespeare banishes Falstaff. But that is to read the novel darkly indeed. For it is preeminently, if not exclusively, the Micawbers who see to it that the hardening discipline in David will never entirely deaden the heart.

To be sure, the matter is not all that symmetrical. The novel ends on an oft-remarked plangent note, on a farewell to youthful comedy and Micawberesque delight and liberty that makes *David Copperfield* Dickens' "Immortality Ode." The comic spirit has been transported with the

Micawbers to Australia, and it is not much consolation that Mr. Micawber occasionally sends back letters full of the old exuberance and extravagant language to enliven the serious paterfamilias and novelist David has become. In contrast, while Murdstone is no longer a factor in David's life, he is still abroad in the land threatening vulnerable young women and their helpless children. Moreover, to the extent that the novel portrays a contest for David's soul between the cash-box ethos of Murdstone and the steaming-punch spirit of Micawber, we are left with the suspicion that the darker rather than the lighter father's values have come to dominate. The mature David can certainly be something of a prig. When he tells us that "the source of my success" is "habits of punctuality, order, and diligence" (ch. 42), do we not hear an echo of Murdstone's sententiousness? And when these habits serve to kill off Dora Spenlow to make room for Agnes Wickfield, that angel in the house whose idealization must have challenged credulity even for the Victorians, do we not have intimations of Murdstone's coldness? It is, at any rate, the upsetting of an earlier balance, the headlong triumph of Dickensian earnestness over Dickensian game, that makes *David Copperfield* in its later pages a highly melancholy book.

But I try not to end on so somber a note. David is not Murdstone; rather, he is the "David Copperfield the Younger" his memory and imagination have combined to create for the title page of his book. In the absence of the father, other characters have tried to usurp the father's naming power, thereby imposing their expectations on David (still another link, I suggest, with Pip—who, however, names himself in the opening chapter of *Great Expectations*). To Murdstone, David is a "Brooks of Sheffield" whose sharpness threatens; to Betsey Trotwood, a renamed "Trotwood" whom she appropriates; to Creakle, a "dog" to be tamed; to the spoiled Steerforth, a "Daisy" whose freshness might save; to Dora, a "Doady" whom she would keep a companionable child. And so on. But by novel's end, David occupies his father's name as human being and artist with full paternal confidence, an author in both senses. "Aut liberi aut libri" 'either children or books,' Nietzsche sadly warns us. David is one of the fortunates who do not have to choose, who, as chapter 64 makes clear, can have it all. So, for that matter, can Dickens (who claimed *David Copperfield* as his "favourite child")—they are both prolific authors of children and books. They have made their marks on the world, they "signify," as the French would put it these days, in both senses.

Such alternative signification, as it relates to the father's and son's competition for the power to name (an issue in several of the course books), is the topic I ask the class to address in their take-home final examination: how does the absence of the father (and we discover that the fathers in all the books we have read are missing from the lives of their children in some crucial way) generate words and/or new lives, the two different forms of signifying? In order to focus that question I outline recent French linguistically oriented theories of narrative desire, of the text or signifier's struggle with and for the paternal signified, and I introduce the students to the opening and closing chapters ("The Discourse of the Father" and "The Discourse of Jacques Lacan") in Robert Con Davis' *The Fictional Father: Lacanian Readings of the Text* (on library reserve). Within that context I describe Dickens' own arduous struggle for the self-mirroring name "David Copperfield" (via "Wellbury," "Flowerbury," "Magbury," "Trotfield," "Trotbury," "Spankle," "Copperboy," "Topflower," and "Copperstone," as he itemizes the way stations [*Letters* 2: 484]). For the author's progress frames the struggle of his protagonist, David Copperfield the Younger, to "make" his name, in the several senses—to wrest the power of nomination from the withholding forces of this "rough world," and to do so by recording that struggle in a book that, ambivalently enough, he (and his author behind him?) "never meant to be Published on any Account" (Frontispiece).

It is, at any rate, something like this that I have in mind when I ask the students to consider in detail at least three of our works in light of the following generalization by Michel Foucault. (While he stresses the father's role in the triggering of psychosis, Foucault's formula seems to be applicable to less extreme psychic disturbances in the son as well.) Because I wish the students to speculate about differences in the role of nomination for "literally" absent and "literally" present biological fathers, I urge (though I do not insist), that they choose *David Copperfield* as one of their evidentiary texts, paying special attention to the italicized sentence. As Foucault writes in "The Father's No,"

> Lacan, following Melanie Klein, has shown that the father, as the third party in the Oedipal situation, is not only the hated and feared rival, but the agent whose presence limits the unlimited relationship between the mother and child and whose first anguished image emerges in the child's fantasy of being devoured. Consequently, the father separates, that is, he is the one who protects when, in his proclamation of the law, he links space, rules, and language within a single and major experience. At a stroke, he creates the distance along which will develop the scansion of presences and absences, the speech whose initial form is based on constraints, and finally, the relationship of the signifier to the signified which not only gives rise to the structure of language but also to the exclusion and symbolic transformation of repressed material. Thus it is not in alimentary or functional terms of deficiency that we understand the gap which now stands in the Father's place. To be able to say that he is missing, that he is hated, excluded, or introjected, that his image has undergone symbolic transmutations, presumes that he is not "foreclosed' (as Lacan would

say) from the start and that his place is not marked by a gaping and absolute emptiness. The father's absence, manifested in the headlong rush of psychosis, is not registered by perceptions or images but relates to the order of the signifier. *The "no" through which this gap is created does not imply the absence of a real individual who bears the father's name; rather it implies that the father has never assumed the role of nomination and that the position of the signifier, through which the father names himself and, according to the Law, through which he is able to name has remained vacant.* It is toward this "no" that the unwavering line of psychosis is infallibly directed; as it is precipitated inside the abyss of meaning, it evokes the devastating absence of the father through the forms of delirium and phantasms and through the catastrophe of the signifier. (81-82; italics added)

David Copperfield: An Introduction to a Dickens Course

Stanley Friedman

When offering a course in Dickens, I assign six novels and open the semester with *David Copperfield*, even though one of the other texts selected, *Oliver Twist*, antedates it by over a decade. For many reasons, Dickens' eighth novel seems especially suitable as an introduction to the reading of his fiction.

Originally published in monthly installments from May 1849 to November 1850, *David Copperfield* stands at what proved the midpoint of its author's career, in the exact center of fifteen novels, if we count the unfinished *Edwin Drood*. Moreover, *Copperfield*, which Dickens acknowledged as his "favourite child" as late as 1867, won for its author the most laudatory critical acclaim of any of his works, according to his friend and biographer John Forster. Indeed, it impressed both Victorian and later readers as retaining the vitality and high-spirited humor of the earlier narratives while simultaneously achieving the stronger unity of structure that Dickens had sought while writing the two immediately preceding novels, *Martin Chuzzlewit* and *Dombey and Son*. This favorable assessment has been sustained (see Adrian), even though no praise would be likely to surpass Tolstoy's assertion: "If you sift the world's prose literature, Dickens will remain; sift Dickens, *David Copperfield* will remain" (quoted in Collins, *Critical Heritage* 242).

By beginning with *Copperfield*, the class and I confront at once what seems the foremost difficulty in studying Dickens, the problem of length. The book is the same size (the one he found most congenial) as the seven other novels that originally appeared in nineteen monthly installments, the last a double number providing half again as much text and twice as many illustrations. To encourage my students to pace themselves sensibly and to read with care, I devote nine fifty-minute class periods to the book and divide the text into nine assignments, each the equivalent of two or three monthly numbers in the original publication: (1) chs. 1-6 (nos. 1-2), (2) chs. 7-12 (nos. 3-4), (3) chs. 13-18 (nos. 5-6), (4) chs. 19-24 (nos. 7-8), (5) chs. 25-34 (nos. 9-11), (6) chs. 35-43 (nos. 12-14), (7) chs. 44-50 (nos. 15-16), (8) chs. 51-57 (nos. 17-18), (9) chs. 58-64 (nos. 19-20).

Such a procedure, somewhat similar to the approach that Michael Lund recommends for various Victorian novels, emphasizes the gradual unfolding of the narrative and seems pedagogically preferable to having the students read a third or half or all of the book by a given date. But this method (which I also use, with some modifications, for the other five works in my course) has one limitation: only in the final class meeting allotted to a specific book can we consider its entire structure. Nevertheless, I have found that, because this system enables students to become relatively familiar with details and aware of the ways in which narrative strands are interwoven, our remarks on the book's overall organization and cohesiveness can be extremely direct and concise. Moreover, for each novel except the last on the reading list, we can appropriate a part of the first period set aside for the next work to be studied.

In a further attempt to ensure close, attentive reading, I usually dictate two or more study questions for the following period's assignment and ask the students to prepare brief written responses (about two hundred to three hundred words) for each query. Although these exercises may be done more informally and less thoroughly than regular papers and are rarely collected, members of the class are expected to consult them during discussions. The responses to these questions can serve as take-off points, and since the class has already thought about the topics involved, the level of commentary seems relatively high.

The questions I dictate are designed to avoid disclosing information that would seriously affect reactions to the text and distort the emphasis Dickens seeks, and in many cases there is no single correct reply. At times, the queries may refer to preceding assignments, so that students must review the portions of the novel completed so far. For almost all of these exercises, I use fairly precise, limited topics, for which secondary materials are neither needed nor, in most instances, particularly helpful. The following are just a few examples, geared to my reading assignments:

For numbers 1-2: In what ways, if any, do the concluding paragraphs of numbers 1 and 2 seem designed to create suspense? Consider the tone of each conclusion, as well as significant likenesses and differences.

For numbers 7-8: Does any scene or incident in chapter 20 seem especially reminiscent of an earlier occurrence described in number 6 (chs. 16-18)? If so, briefly mention important parallels and contrasts.

For numbers 9-11: In what specific ways have the major events in chapter 31 ("A Greater Loss") been anticipated by David in the preceding sections of his narrative?

For numbers 12-14: How do Mrs. Crupp and Mr. Spenlow, who are introduced in earlier numbers, seem alike? Consider personality, behavior, and the relationship that each figure has with David.

For numbers 15-16: In what ways does the fifth paragraph in chapter 47 ("Martha") use specific details to create a mood? Consider diction, syntax, and imagery. How is this atmosphere related to the events described just after?

Students who respond to these queries with care find pleasure in noticing the extraordinary intricacy with which elements in the text are interwoven, for minor touches often seem related to larger matters. This feature can be illustrated by a synthesis of some responses to the question concerning parallels between two lesser characters, Mrs. Crupp and Mr. Spenlow.

David first meets both in chapter 23, which describes his departure from the direct supervision of his "second mother," Aunt Betsey, after leaving the school run by the fatherly Dr. Strong. Mrs. Crupp, from whom David rents rooms, indicates that "she should always yearn towards" him "as a son" (ch. 23) and stresses that she is a mother herself (chs. 26, 34). Spenlow, the proctor to whom David is articled, is a paternal figure not only because of his role as employer but also because he becomes a prospective father-in-law after the protagonist's secret engagement to Dora (ch. 33). Both Mrs. Crupp and Spenlow, however, turn out to be false parental surrogates, for they are denying and deceitful. Mrs. Crupp evades work (chs. 24, 28), while Spenlow uses Mr. Jorkins, his partner, as an excuse for charging a high premium and refusing David any salary (ch. 23). Although the youthful David would benefit from wise guidance as he seeks maturity, neither Mrs. Crupp's counsel on wooing (ch. 26) nor Spenlow's advice on his profession (chs. 26, 33) seems particularly valuable. David appears awed by Spenlow, however, and also refers to enduring the "tyranny" of Mrs. Crupp (ch. 28). Interestingly, both of these dominating figures suffer from physical maladies, Mrs. Crupp being a "martyr to a curious disorder called 'the spazzums,'" which calls for brandy as a remedy (ch. 26), and Mr. Spenlow being "in the habit of complaining of pains in his head" (ch. 38). After Aunt Betsey claims to be financially ruined, Spenlow is unwilling to let David cancel his articles (ch. 35), while Mrs. Crupp objects to his giving up his rooms at an early date (ch. 35).

Mrs. Crupp's negative influence wanes, however, after Aunt Betsey and Peggotty, true mother surrogates, arrive in London, and the landlady seems to disappear from David's view in number 12, when she takes to hiding in the kitchen, terrified of Miss Trotwood, who has deliberately given the "impression" of being "mad" (ch. 37). In the next chapter, which begins number 13, Spenlow suddenly dies. Before this, David has started work as a part-time secretary to a true father figure, Dr. Strong (ch. 36). The many parallels between the landlady and the proctor perhaps convince us that these two are more significant than they at first appeared, for their deceitful, ungenerous traits emphasize the opposite qualities in characters who do assist David.

Although the foregoing analysis is more complete than the response written by any one student, most of the points are usually brought up by the class collectively. By doing these exercises conscientiously, class members can gauge the extent of their understanding, prepare themselves to partici-pate effectively in discussions, and begin accumulating material helpful for purposes of review and sometimes for writing the extended essays that I assign later. In addition, I occasionally select three students during the period prior to a given class meeting and ask them to initiate our considera-tion of a particular problem by reading from or talking about their replies to a study question. The trio speaks for ten to fifteen minutes, and then their classmates and I join the conversation.

Of course, *David Copperfield*, besides presenting the problem of length, also includes various other features that make it desirable as a starting novel. As Dickens' most autobiographical book it introduces us not only to many details about his childhood and later years but also to his artistic use of what I call his emotional history. During the first meeting of the semester, I refer to John Forster's biography and other sources in order to review briefly Dickens' life up to the writing of *David Copperfield*, emphasizing five events that markedly affected him: his brief employment as a twelve-year-old in a blacking warehouse, the three-month imprisonment of his father for debt, the rejection by Maria Beadnell, the sudden death of his sister-in-law Mary Hogarth, and the loss, many years later, of his older sister Fanny. Although the last occurrence has received less attention than the other four, it moved Dickens deeply, recalling his early attachment to Fanny. Her demise, in September 1848, shortly before he began planning *David Copperfield*, may have contributed to this novel's persistent emphasis on mortality.

The traces in *Copperfield* of numerous biographical materials have been examined by many scholars, including Edgar Johnson (*Tragedy and Triumph*), William Oddie, and Philip Collins ("Interweaving of Truth and Fiction"). But, despite the value of this novel in illustrating its author's fictional adaptation of his personal history, in my course I give greater attention to how *Copperfield* serves as a guide to other facets of Dickens' art.

During class sessions, we study the manner in which the narrative unfolds from installment to installment and also notice the use of recurrent images, motifs, situations, and phrases; the effects of settings on figures in the story and on us; the techniques employed to interweave different plot strands; the pairing and contrasting of characters; and the construction of scenes. For example, we consider—without anticipating sections not yet reached by students reading the novel for the first time—the gradual development of three major plot lines: David's survival of the Murdstone threat and his subsequent relationships with Dora and Agnes (a strand that could itself be divided into three); Steerforth's seduction of Em'ly; and Heep's scheming against the Wickfields. Interwoven with these are such minor threads as the tribulations of the Micawbers, the problems of the Strongs, and the financial difficulties of Aunt Betsey.

I emphasize the novel's concern with David's responses to adversity and with his attempts to understand his own preceding life. In doing so, I follow some of the approaches developed in my essay "Dickens' Mid-Victorian Theodicy: *David Copperfield*," asking the class to examine the ways in which the book explores (1) the question of human control over events, (2) the problem of death, and (3) the hope of providential comfort. For me, the narrative presents David's ultimate triumph in overcoming difficulties, especially those attributable to three villains—Murdstone, Steerforth, and Heep—each of whom affects the protagonist by preying on a woman with whom he is in some way involved. Through much of the novel, Agnes plays a major, beneficent role, leading David to comprehend the importance of religious faith. I find that focusing on Dickens' main themes brings out more clearly the value of the narrative's later sections and helps sustain my students' interest.

In class discussions, I encourage students to explore interrelations among characters and also among events. For instance, in the sixth installment we encounter two mysterious details: the loss of Annie Strong's "cherry-colored ribbon," which raises questions about her fidelity (ch. 16), and Mr. Dick's claim that a stranger "hides" near the house of Aunt Betsey and frightens her (ch. 17). Much later (no. 15), the first of these mysteries is resolved, when Mr. Dick, who introduced the second problem, arranges the situation leading to Annie's convincing defense of her loyalty (ch. 45). In the succeeding number, the other puzzle is clarified, for we learn that the stranger, whom David has seen (ch. 23), is Aunt Betsey's husband (ch. 47). Moreover, my students notice a minor link between Jack Maldon, who exposes Annie to Heep's slanderous accusations, and Aunt Betsey's husband: they both go to India; this location ties together two men who are physically attractive, financially shiftless, and inclined to prey on women. The clear implication is that Jack would have been a husband much like Betsey Trotwood's. But since the information that Betsey's husband moved to India appears only in the first chapter, while Maldon's departure for the same destination is not mentioned until number 6, published five months later, only an exceptionally attentive reader would see the connection and appreciate its full extent. In effect, we treat *David Copperfield* as an enormous poem that magnificently integrates many diverse elements. Of course, the idea that Dickens is "one of the great poets of the novel" (Edgar Johnson, "Dark Pilgrimage" 42) has been considered by various scholars, including John Speirs and Carl Dawson.

During our last meeting devoted to *Copperfield*, I point out another advantage of using it to start our course: it contains especially fine examples of nearly all the features that we usually associate with Dickens' fiction, of themes and techniques present in both earlier and later books. I ask students to take note of the following Dickensian characteristics: the interweaving of several plot strands; the numerous climaxes that appear in various places (especially in the central parts—called the "keystone" by William Axton [34]—and the last few installments of each work); the inclusion of both tragic and comic elements; the large number of characters (in each of the eight longer novels, thirty to fifty relatively memorable figures); the employment of both urban and rural settings; an insistence on coincidences that establish links or evoke wonder; a concern with final testaments; one or more prison scenes; a serious illness suffered by the protagonist; benevolent and malevolent manipulators; sexual misconduct, treated in a circumspect manner; topical references to social issues (e.g., in *Copperfield*, prostitution, emigration to Australia, and "model prisons"); an interest in situations and characters that reflect basic anxieties or desires: the orphan or defenseless child, the improvident or abusive parental figure, the generous "godparent," the dying infant or young person, the kind (and perhaps wise) fool, the devoted servant, the ardent male suitor, the idealized sisterly figure, the beautiful yet silly or coquettish young woman, the ogre or extreme villain (deceptive and greedy), moral tests, and sudden changes of fortune—all of these being elements associated with fairy tales and melodrama; caricatures or eccentrics; characters who seem invested with mythic significance (like Mr. Peggotty, especially in ch. 40, "The Wanderer"); mysteries and surprises; passages of moralistic commentary by the narrator and other characters; and a conclusive ending that provides capsule remarks on the fates, often poetically just, of many characters. Indeed, this list fully supports the idea in the title of a stimulating essay by Richard J. Dunn—"*David Copperfield*: All Dickens Is There."

My students' pleasure seems greatly enhanced by the fact that close study of *David Copperfield* enables and prompts them to observe unusually interesting resemblances and contrasts to the five additional novels in the course. For instance, when we go backward in Dickens' career to read *Oliver Twist*, the class finds in that book's hero an orphan who overcomes difficulties even greater than those facing David. They also discover in Nancy an anticipation of the later narrative's concern with prostitution, and they may compare the juxtaposition in *Oliver Twist* of tragic and comic elements (a technique explicitly referred to in ch. 17) to the same practice in *Copperfield*.

After *Oliver Twist*, we proceed to *Bleak House*, the work written directly after *David Copperfield* and the only Dickens novel besides it and *Great Expectations* to make sustained use of a first-person narrator. In the chapters presented by Esther Summerson, she briefly describes her childhood as an orphan, under a Murdstone-like regimen, and later tells of her adoption by a benevolent eccentric who, like Aunt Betsey, offers protection, guidance, and love. Although *Bleak House* gives more attention to specific social issues than *Copperfield* does, we may recall that the earlier work includes some mild satire on matters like wills and Parliament.

One theme found in both *David Copperfield* and *Bleak House*—marital disharmony—also links them with the next novel in my course, *Hard Times*. Then, too, David's list of great books that sustained him during the Murdstone period points to the worth of imagination as an aid in life, a theme developed in *Hard Times*. This narrative, of course, strongly repudiates Gradgrind's hostility to fancy, an antipathy reminiscent of the Small-weeds' opposition to fiction (*Bleak House*, ch. 21). Among other connections between *Copperfield* and *Hard Times* are various resemblances between Bitzer and Heep and also between James Harthouse and James Steerforth.

From *Hard Times*, we move to *Great Expectations*, a first-person narrative by a hero whom Dickens described to John Forster as "a boy-child, like David." While starting to write this book, Dickens reread *Copperfield* in order to avoid "unconscious repetitions" (Forster, Ley ed., 734). But despite—or perhaps because of—this precaution, the later novel includes a great number of parallels (many of which may not have been consciously intended), as well as intriguing contrasts. Comments on the Pip-David, Miss Havisham-Aunt Betsey, Biddy-Agnes, and Herbert-Traddles relationships, as well as other pairings, are offered by many scholars (e.g., Buckley; Pearlman; Stone, *Invisible World*).

To conclude my course, we read Dickens' last completed novel, *Our Mutual Friend*. Among the links that especially interest my students are those between Steerforth and Eugene Wrayburn (the latter is much more bound by conscience in his dealings with an attractive woman from the lower classes) and between Heep and Silas Wegg (two scheming, grasping hypocrites who overreach themselves and are denounced in comic exposure scenes).

During the semester, my students seem especially to enjoy studying not only the similarities and differences between *Copperfield* and each of the additional novels but also the interrelations among these five other books. By starting the course with *David Copperfield* and suggesting its centrality in the Dickens canon, I attempt to help my students acquire an enthusiastic interest in his many skills as artist, moralist, and observer of humanity.

SPECIFIC APPROACHES

David Copperfield's "Written Memory"

Jean Ferguson Carr

David Copperfield calls his project of recalling and structuring his life "my written memory" (ch. 48), and he devotes much of his attention to how his imagination weaves strands of experience and memory into a meaningful whole. David's deliberations about his creative processes make the novel a particularly appropriate text for teaching literature and writing together, for raising significant questions about language and narration. The issues of writing, or words as objects, and of documents and narratives permeate the novel. David is writing his autobiography and learning to be a novelist, and he traces his growth partially through his deep involvement with the written word. David develops as an author in a world where writing projects often seem obsessive and solipsistic and where self-knowledge seems a crucial precondition for writing something with the "power of doing good" (ch. 60). His story suggests the difficult gap between public and private meanings and provides students with a focus for discussing language's power and limitations, its potential as inventive force and protective cover.

David Copperfield offers several different levels for exploring the reading and writing of texts and worlds. David's efforts to call back the "phantoms" of the past (ch. 4), to sort out and order the fluid elements of memory, serve as an intriguing case study in autobiographical writing, in how one defines or creates a self through language and narrative strategies. His practice of structuring his memory around a particular object can be used as an exemplary model for students learning to appreciate and write descriptive or narrative prose. The novel, however, does not offer an unqualified or static portrait of David as an artist; instead, Dickens shows how his character's awareness of autobiographical issues changes as he matures and as he learns from the experiences of others. The novel is useful, therefore, in developing a critical attitude toward the processes of writing and reading a life and toward the written work, whether the subject is the past, the self, or something that seems initially less vulnerable to the writer's shaping power. The problems of choice and structure that Dickens (or David) faces are significant for all writers.

I use *David Copperfield* to introduce a course on autobiography in which students read nonfictional lives (Mill, Trollope, Wilde, Douglass, Twain, Woolf, Kingston, and excerpts from others) and fictional lives (Margaret Atwood's *Surfacing*, Tillie Olsen's "I Stand Here Ironing," poems from John Berryman's *Dream Songs*, excerpts from Wordsworth's *The Prelude* and Carlyle's *Sartor Resartus*). They write critical and creative assignments. The course, offered as an elective for students beyond the first year, has attracted English majors with a fairly wide range of literary and creative experience as well as nonmajors taking their first course in the humanities. Most students enter the course expecting that the reading and writing will be relatively undemanding, that they can be anecdotal and confessional—in short, personal. The novel satisfies many of their initial goals and interests, but it also challenges their previous assumptions about remembering and constructing a self. Starting with *Copperfield*—a novelist's creation of a character who narrates his autobiography—encourages students to consider the choices made, the other lives available to be remembered or created, and it lets them begin to transfer such issues from the realm of fiction to that of nonfiction. The length of the book becomes a pedagogical advantage, allowing students to set forth problems in reading, writing, and evaluating autobiography through their involvement with David's changing processes and through their own efforts to apply his strategies. The novel offers a valuable context for discussing the uses and misuses of language and narrative in communicating a life and a past.

David is surrounded by negative models: characters who rely on writing or declaiming as a retreat from active participation in the world, who use language to replace reality rather than to represent or improve it. Words still fascinate and preoccupy people, but they seem to lack the power to communicate. The novel's presentation of wasteful and directionless repetition is a gentler version of the language in *Great Expectations*, which has lost its currency from malicious misuse and so has become a "spurious coin" forged for deception and harm (ch. 28). Instead of emerging from a careful perception of the self and the past, writing in David's world seems primarily an emblem of mental distraction. It fails to address a profound sense of the world and its problems or of readers' needs; indeed, many of the writers seem content to repeat their words to no effect, to fly pages of the Memorial on kites or to write endless letters to uncaring recipients. Dr. Strong's work preparing the sourcebook for language, the Dictionary, is presented as an endless task that blinds its creator to serious obscurities in human meanings and motives. To be fully useful, he must awaken from his dream of language, learn to read his world with "new meaning," and attempt to save his wife—not just his words—from "misconstruction" (ch. 42). Mr. Dick poses the ultimate problems of the writer: he can never get his subject "quite right" or make it "perfectly clear" (ch. 14). His obsession, which traps him in frustrating repetition (see Westburg), limits his effectiveness in the world and shows David the necessity of confronting, not just entertaining, the ghosts of the mind.

David's strategies for recalling and shaping his past show his imaginative control, sensitivity to language, and anxiety about the truthfulness and value of his product. Wary of adults' tendencies to rationalize or revise experience, he tries to recall details from his childhood that will authenticate his interpretations of his life. David attempts to give his version of the past validity and force by describing his memories as almost physical sensations that left a real rather than an imagined mark on his sensitive mind. When he tries to describe his memory of his old nurse Peggotty's roughened finger, for example, it is almost as if the finger had touched his memory as well as his child's hand or face: "I have an impression on my mind which I cannot distinguish from actual remembrance, of the touch of Peggotty's forefinger" (ch. 2). David the adult narrator tries to recapture this childhood "objectivity" by making associations between present and past images. He focuses on physical objects that he claims trigger scenes buried in his memory, like the ring "associated in my remembrance with Dora's hand" that causes a "momentary stirring in my heart, like pain!" (ch. 33) or the storm that kills Ham and Steerforth, which is so "indelibly" etched in his memory that he can get it back "at the lightest mention of a sea-shore" (ch. 55). David describes these physical associations as if they enable him to evoke the past without language or narrative; he often narrates the past they call up in the present tense, as if he were actually transported back instead of trying to present it in words in the present. Yet David also self-consciously marks this road to his past as he lives it; he often seems to assign significance to objects as he lives so he can recall them significantly as he writes.

Students who try to imitate David's methods of generating his past through a train of associations with objects experience the difficulty of balancing private and public realms. Much skill and thought is involved in constructing what may seem an "actual remembrance," in writing perceptive self-revelations, and in making them illuminating to an audience. One can emphasize the success of David's strategies by contrasting them with the vacuous generalities, predetermined questions ("Must not D.C. confine himself to the broad pinions of Time?"), and conventional images ("Are tears the dewdrops of the heart?") that fill Julia Mills's diary (ch. 38). Julia's comic failure suggests the limitations of clichéd emblems of memory, objects—like the first toy, the Christmas tree, the class ring, or the family snapshot album—that mark out public or generic development rather than individual pasts. One student writing an autobiographical sketch struggled to make his private associations with popular records come to life for his classmates; his audience either did not know the records or knew them all too well and too personally. That student searched the novel for scenes that rely on common experiences for their impact and yet are vivid and particular, like David's childhood pleasure with his crocodile book or the catalog of smells that recall his schoolroom ("mildewed corduroys, sweet apples wanting air, and rotten books" [ch. 9]).

Another student wanted to work through the problem Dickens raises of appearing too self-consciously manipulative of memories. She chose a forgotten, ordinary object as the structuring link for her past and present to make the associations seem revealing instead of simply contrived to reveal. The object did not have a predetermined symbolic meaning, but was infused with meaning through her process of writing about it. To evoke her sense of having left the warmth and continuity of her family she focused on the keys to her house, which were no longer useful since the house had been sold but which she still kept. Just as David uses the smell of leaves or the seashore to move himself rhetorically back to his past, so this student used keys as a trigger for visual memories (the image of them hanging by the door or hidden in her suitcase), for personal memories (the stories of how her grandfather gave her the keys and her sisters lost them), and as a link to her present (her discovery of the keys in a desk drawer in her new apartment). She had learned the power of evoking the act of remembering, as well as the remembered past; she gave her narrative a purpose beyond private nostalgia and made her audience care about how her past had shaped her present narrating self.

These reading and writing experiences make students more sensitive to issues faced by all writers but especially evident in autobiographical writing. They see the imaginative value of David's strategies but also the problems Dickens poses for his character, problems David often represses or resists. In his *Autobiography*, Yeats wrote that he was wary of writing a book about himself "for to do that is to exchange life for a logical process" (311). Indeed one aspect of *David Copperfield* that students criticized was its constant valuing of the verbal or literary self. Students who delighted in David's childhood grew somewhat restless over what they saw as a more static, self-congratulatory adult life. David recognizes he may be suspected of using his narrative powers to obscure his past. "I write the exact truth," he claims. "It would avail me nothing to extenuate it now" (ch. 44). But the issue clearly extends beyond any deliberate attempt to falsify the past; the difficulty is how an autobiographer knows or writes "the exact truth" and how fully the written life can approach the lived experience. David makes a compact to "reflect [his] mind on the paper, [to] examine it, closely, and bring its secrets to light" (ch. 48). As students can experience in their own writing endeavors, David's simplifying term "reflect" conceals a world of effort. He will more nearly approach "the exact truth" by becoming self-conscious and critical about the shaping power of his adult, remembering, writing self, about the metaphors by which he "represents" his past and himself.

David's development as a writer and the experience of "retracing" his steps (ch. 31) lead him to greater self-consciousness about his process of shaping his material. David does not fully welcome this maturity, because he sees it also as a loss of childhood's innocent delight in words as objects. He must work harder to recapture the time when words recalled "no feeling of disgust or reluctance," when he delighted simply in the "fat black letters in the primer, the puzzling novelty of their shapes, and the easy good-nature of O and Q and S" (ch. 4). And he dreads the pain that writing can bring, the memories of betrayal and loss that may emerge with the delight. He suggests that the writing of such sorrows makes them "indelible" (ch. 55) and that, like the past itself, the "remembrance" of the past "is fraught with so much pain" (ch. 14). Yet he also recognizes that such times are lost forever without the mediative effect of language. Only through a verbal command—"Let me remember how it used to be" (ch. 4)—can he approach the past. David's desire to recapture some measure of his past begins to overcome his need to partition off or repress sorrow (see Gilmour and Horton). Dickens shows him using his writer's skill and his sense of creating a significant narrative to raise the secret "curtains" of his life (ch. 14).

Students can trace David's various strategies for writing the past, contrasting scenes in which he calls attention to his art with those in which he asks permission to "stand aside" as narrator (ch. 43). These "Retrospect" chapters—such as chapter 14, in which he describes himself as a ghostly director or magician "calling up" players from the past and raising and lowering the curtain on the scene that passes before him—suggest a distanced and passive narrator, a writer who appears as audience or reader of a scene. He regularly portrays himself as an observer of his own life—a strange little boy off to one side watching while adults argue over his fate or a strange adult hiding behind doors while other adults take central roles in crisis scenes. David links his ability to evoke retrospects to his childhood, preverbal ability to "observe, in little pieces" without "making a net of a number of these pieces" (ch. 2). The "Retrospect" chapters are set off, by authorial command, from the narrated story; they are given the objective weight of the child's unprejudiced observations. But Dickens shows that David, like all writers, manufactures his "net" more deliberately than he admits. Students learn from David's story that all scenes, no matter how magically evoked by an invisible director, are constructed, offered through some particular narrative metaphor (as image, or drama, or written verification), and that the narrator assumes a particular relationship to the events being described. This alters the emphasis from "what happens" to "how we are told it": students can thus become more sophisticated in discussing the fiction-making choices of an author or narrator and in considering their own rhetorical stances as writers. They focus on metaphors for presentation, seeing details not merely as "out there" but as mediated by an involved teller, a desired conclusion, or an expected result.

Students can thus learn to criticize their own reading and writing. They can assess David's claims that as a child he had the power to blend words and things, a power that he feels gives him, as an adult, an objective authority in narrating events. His assertions that objects convey meanings to him and that words can be objectively verified and controlled contrast with his recognition of those memories words cannot call up or alter. For much of the book, David seems to feel he can report language and imagination as features of the external, verifiable world. Because his sense of reality is so seamless (or, we might argue, inverted, since his imagination seems more real), words and stories can serve as both pieces of concrete evidence and the medium of proof. The child delights in hearing Peggotty speak of her nephew Ham as "a morsel of English Grammar" (ch. 2); the adult risks taking the written life as sufficient, settling for an orderly but utterly fictional self. In chapter 63, David describes his structuring of the material as weaving, a metaphor that suggests the power of the adult's imagination to make strong connections, find a meaningful "thread," and link parts into a whole. But the metaphor also counters David's earlier insistence on a truly objective narrative (ch. 2) and suggests the motive of catching or trapping. David's metaphor echoes John Stuart Mill's earnest efforts in his *Autobiography* to piece together the "fabric of [his] old and taught opinions" (163). Like Mill, who blended the art of writing with the process of experiencing the life—"I never allowed it to fall to pieces, but was incessantly occupied in weaving it anew" (163)—David structures his life, both lived and written. The comparison with Mill suggests that David's strategies are also defenses, that he must use his writing abilities to soften the harshness of his past, to revise his life.

David's story explores the manifold difficulties and possibilities of writing a life, of creating a "written memory." His wistful melancholy on the limits of using language to recreate his past world is a recurring concern in Dickens' novels, in his failed autobiographical efforts and self-revealing letters, and, of course, in Romantic and Victorian autobiographical writing from Wordsworth and Mill to *Jane Eyre* or *Sartor Resartus*. *David Copperfield*'s exploration of the ambivalent powers of language and its presentation of the ties between self-knowledge and knowledge of the world offer students thematic and critical approaches to the Victorian period. Dickens suggests that David's longing for that preverbal, preexperiential past can become, as it has for many other autobiographers, a barrier to his growth and usefulness as an adult, a barrier reconfirmed or overcome through his writing. If his writing is to have therapeutic value for himself and his society, David must learn the functions and malfunctions of writing. His imaginative power to bring forth memories with the vividness of present experience must be tempered by an adult awareness of the art involved. Words are not things but signs by which people struggle to communicate, and that struggle must aim for something more than a nostalgic retreat into a fictional world. If the child is to be father to the man rather than a perpetual child like Micawber or Mr. Dick, he must direct his most serious personal issues out to the world and must tolerate a critical response from his adult self. David's writing can thus become a way to free him from obsessive repetition of his past and move him beyond egocentric concerns. His story encourages sophisticated self-consciousness about language and writing, in both their literary and their social uses.

Dickens' portrait of David as autobiographer offers students a model of a skilled, sensitive writer using an exploration of his past to delight, entertain, and instruct (to paraphrase one of David's most enthusiastic readers, Mr. Micawber [ch. 63]). But perhaps more importantly, Dickens and his readers can use David's experiences to explore the value and difficulty of writing autobiography. David's ambivalence about making painful memories indelible through his skill is an important experience for beginning writers who are themselves scared of appearing shallow or silly in their writing, whether it is directly autobiographical or not. David's complex search for strategies to approximate the past in words also reassures students who suspect too much analysis will destroy their personal or emotional selves. Focusing on autobiography is a delicate experience for teacher and students, but it also allows students to combine their private and public concerns, their intellectual and emotional lives, in a significant and shared inquiry. It encourages them to consider interpretive understanding important in their education beyond the English class and to think of writing as more than a mechanical transaction.

"I have taken with fear and trembling to authorship": *David Copperfield* in the Composition Classroom

Melissa Sue Kort

Admittedly, ulterior motives influenced my first considering *David Copperfield* as the sole reading text for a community college class that combined first-year and remedial composition students. I wanted a chance to teach a Victorian novel almost as much as I wanted my students to write better essays. Some colleagues thought I was crazy: the book was long and old-fashioned; I was teaching composition, not literature; I would have to force-feed Dickens to people who thought good stories solved the problems of the world in ninety minutes or less and came with commercial breaks.

I firmly believe that the only real subject in a composition course is writing; this was not going to become a class in Dickens. I felt fairly safe, since I dedicate more than half of my composition classroom time to one-on-one tutorials (following Roger Garrison's method as advocated in his *How a Writer Works*). The more I looked at the novel in terms of the writing text I had already used in conjunction with other reading (Ken Macrorie's *Telling Writing*), and the more I thought about the objectives of my writing class, the more I realized that Dickens embodied most of what is good and bad in writing. And despite his weighty reputation (he was already branded "untouchable" by most of my students), he wrote as a popular novelist. Could he still control a less willing audience a century later? By the time they reached the section describing young David's return to Blunderstone Rookery after his first visit to Yarmouth, my students were hooked, and our discussions on writing had already found a common model, scapegoat, and source of both confusion and delight.

Before the students started reading the novel or writing, we needed to determine criteria for effective writing. Macrorie encourages criticism of even "great literature":

> Writing is good not because of who writes it or where it appears. Shakespeare and William Faulkner have written badly at times, and good publishers have marketed bad work. Writing is good because of what it says, how it opens up a world of ideas or facts for readers. And how accurately and memorably it speaks, a voice issuing from a human being who is fascinating, surprising, illuminating. But still a man and a writer who does not always strike sparks.
>
> Most good writing is clear, vigorous, honest, alive, sensuous, appropriate, unsentimental, rhythmic, without pretension, fresh, metaphorical, evocative in sound, economical, authoritative, suprising, memorable, and light. (21)

Copperfield would be all that, I promised, and when it wasn't, we would examine where, how, and maybe even why Dickens failed. This method would help us avoid the same errors and would also allow my students to take chances, to try fresh phrases or play with language, even to risk making mistakes—all essential to the improvement of their writing.

Macrorie offers a useful checklist of ways in which good writings gain their power:

1. They do not waste words.
2. They speak in an authentic voice.
3. They put readers there, make them believe.
4. They cause things to happen for them as they happened for the writer (narrator).
5. They create oppositions which pay off in surprise.
6. They build.
7. They ask something of readers.
8. They reward them with meaning. (24)

For us, all these categories served a double purpose—to judge and improve our own writing and to judge and appreciate Dickens'. I divided the novel into its original monthly parts and I spread the readings in *Telling Writing* over the first month of class. I never actually sat down to coordinate the two books, but no matter what Macrorie condemned or condoned, the section we were reading in *David Copperfield* had at least one passage to support his views. After Macrorie attacked sentimentality, for example, my students arrived at class moaning over some mushy scene. The serendipitous emergence of such connections further reinforced my confidence in using the novel.

Telling Writing suggests a variety of writing tasks, beginning with description and narration and drawing heavily on the writers' childhood memories. I selected Dickens partly because few writers depict the child's point of view as well, and I thought *David Copperfield* appropriate because it makes extensive use of Dickens' own memories and records the life of a writer in first person.

Each class began with a "freewrite" (writing for ten minutes without stopping or worrying about mechanics), responding to topics I'd put on the board. Sometimes I asked for a response to the novel so I could keep tabs on my students' reading and stimulate discussion. Since I required one essay on the novel, without giving a specific topic, I encouraged students to use their freewrites for ideas. Sometimes I asked them to imitate something Dickens had done: describe your first day at a new school; describe your first time drunk. When I felt their reading was falling behind, I gave pop quizzes that concentrated on details: Who is " 'umble"? What is the crocodile book? Who cries, "Janet, donkeys!"? I wanted to be sure that my students recognized Dickens' "telling facts," as Macrorie calls them, so that they could see the effect of piling on so many concrete images.

To strengthen my students' awareness of the novel as a masked autobiography, I brought in videotaped segments from the PBS production *Dickens of London*. This also helped accustom them to Dickens' language. I photocopied the autobiographical fragment pertaining to Dickens' experience in the blacking factory. Richard Long's *National Geographic* article "The England of Charles Dickens" gave my nonreaders a better picture of the world I was asking them to enter. Dickens in *National Geographic*? That brought a few more stragglers into the fold.

To establish a clear need for studying Dickens, I attempted to convince my students that Dickens permeates our society's consciousness. If they could recognize the broad cultural repercussions of knowing and appreciating great works of literature, I reasoned, then perhaps they would be more motivated to sharpen both their reading and, more important in my class, their writing. We attended a local production of *A Christmas Carol* and collected newspaper and magazine advertisements that evoked Dickensian ideas of Christmas. I told the story of the near riot in New York harbor after the crowds learned of the death of Little Nell, and one of my students presented me with a plate she had found at the local flea market depicting the Old Curiosity Shop, with Nell peeking out of the window. Others found torn or treasured volumes of Dickens tucked away in the family library or attic. We often read passages aloud in class and talked about how the first readers experienced the novels (this also gave me a chance to catch slower readers and offer special help). A student brought in an old family cookbook that explained how to prepare certain foods mentioned in *David Copperfield*; we took pity on Dora. All this activity brought Dickens off the dusty shelves and reinforced the reading experience.

In teaching writing, I focus on revision rather than on rules or exercises. Students bring drafts of essays to in-class tutorials, at which I quickly read the essays, and then make specific suggestions for improvement. When I used *David Copperfield*, I often referred students to passages in the novel to make a point about a problem or to clarify a suggestion. At the beginning of the semester, when most students were writing descriptions and narrations, I found this approach particularly useful in helping them understand the effect of carefully chosen details. Sometimes, I confess, I went too far. One day in tutorial, I was explaining to a Saudi student that his floating in abstractions without ever landing on a concrete image made his essay very difficult to follow. "Look at Dickens," I advised him. "See how he uses concrete details." "But Dickens is Dickens," my student replied, with all the wisdom of the East in his voice, "and Mahmoud is Mahmoud." I learned to curb my enthusiasm.

Beginning a writing class by encouraging narrative and descriptive essays always causes a problem—helping students shift into argument, persuasion, and other more strictly expository modes without losing the skills developed in writing narrations and descriptions. Using the novel eased the transition. I didn't have to resort to model essays that discussed only marginally interesting topics. Instead, I brought in essays by writers from a variety of fields, talking about different aspects of Dickens or of *David Copperfield.*

I began with Virginia Woolf's short appreciation of the novel, collected in *The Moment and Other Essays.* She both chastises and compliments Dickens, noting that, among other faults, he seems incapable of dealing with mature emotions (*"David Copperfield"* 77). My class discussed this criticism in the light of the passages Woolf mentions, and then we talked about problems in writing about our own mature (and not so mature) emotions. A discussion on subjectivity and objectivity ensued. Not suprisingly, most of the topics and issues that make up any conventional composition course arose, unforced, from discussions of the novel, often without my conscious planning. And because the pictures the novel drew and the sheer pleasure of reading the story involved the students more than a rhetoric manual would have, I believe those lessons were more firmly implanted.

Woolf also stresses that the most valuable effect of Dickens' works is that "They make creators of us all and not merely readers and spectators" (78). She thus supports Macrorie's claim that good writings "cause things to happen for [the reader] as they happened for the writer." We discussed techniques for involving the reader more, particularly in essays that aimed at arguing and proving rather than just showing and telling.

The *Copperfield* esssay led to two other Woolf pieces, "Craftsmanship" and "Professions for Women," collected in *Death of the Moth and Other Essays.* These essays provided a brief respite from Dickens, while still focusing on writing, and they also introduced my students to another first-rate author. Looking at three essays by the same author gave us a chance to discuss another style, Victorian in origin but strictly modern in essence.

Because my students are not primarily English majors or even liberal arts majors, I employed as many cross-disciplinary approaches as possible. I brought in George Orwell's essay "Charles Dickens," which characterizes Dickens' criticism of society as morally rather than politically sound. Orwell renders in detail the social background of many of Dickens' polemics and devotes large sections to *David Copperfield.* The essay opened a discussion of Dickens as crusader and also exposed my students to his other novels.

Orwell does not ignore Dickens' writing style. "When one reads any strongly individual piece of writing," Orwell notes, "one has the impression of seeing a face somewhere behind the page" (73). Macrorie describes the phenomenon as hearing "an authentic voice" (24). We looked at some students' essays and tried to picture the "face . . . behind the page."

"Politics and the English Language" followed. Dickens probably would have shared Orwell's concern about the inherently political danger of slovenly, inaccurate language, my students decided, but because of the pressures of publication, his incurable sentimentality, or his sheer pleasure in letting lovely language flow from his pen, he wasn't able to comply with Orwell's dictates. We talked about what Macrorie calls "Engfish," the pretentious language of the schools, and about curing the urge to write merely what the teacher wants. We discussed techniques for tightening prose and I borrowed freely from Richard Lanham's "Paramedic Method" as described in *Revising Prose*.

Our discussion of tightening naturally turned to Mr. Micawber's verbosity; David's cry, "I wallow in words," when he begins his parliamentary recording career (ch. 42); and his later "talk about the tyranny of words," when he reflects on the legal language Micawber so relishes (ch. 52). I brought in an essay on legal jargon, David S. Levine's "My Client Has Discussed Your Proposal to Fill the Drainage Ditch with His Partners." Levine describes the linguistic result of the search for legal precedents as "a tyranny of words and phrases canned by compilers" (405). Students jumped at the recognition. After legal jargon we talked about the jargons of other professions and interest groups, a discussion to which my students, who came from a variety of backgrounds and majors, contributed enthusiastically. Some attempted essays defining particular jargons or slang.

Because most of my students are more familiar with movies than with books, I always try to emphasize visual as well as verbal literacy in my classes, and *David Copperfield* helped me connect the two. Encouraging careful "reading" of films can encourage and improve the reading of books. To promote better film viewing and to enhance students' appreciation of Dickens, I assigned excerpts from Sergei Eisenstein's "Dickens, Griffith, and the Film Today." Eisenstein traces "the first shoots of the American film esthetic" to Dickens and the Victorian novel, detailing how director D.W. Griffith developed some of his revolutionary film techniques, including close-ups and the narration of parallel stories, from his understanding of Dickens (195). Eisenstein also makes broader, often political connections between film and Dickens, seeing in their common elements—"method, style, and especially in viewpoint and exposition"—part of the reason why both enjoyed mass success.

> What were the novels of Dickens for his contemporaries, for his readers? There is one answer: they bore the same relationship to them that the film bears to the same strata in our time. They compelled the reader to live with the same passions. They appealed to the same good and sentimental elements as does the film (at least on the surface); they alike shudder before vice, they alike mill the extraordi-

nary, the unusual, the fantastic, from boring, prosaic and everyday existence. And they clothe this common and prosaic existence in their special vision. (206)

This assignment goes beyond Woolf's recognition of Dickens' "visualizing power to the extreme" ("*David Copperfield*" 79) or Orwell's belief that "When Dickens has once described something, you see it for the rest of your life" (47). Dickens keeps our vision moving and directs it carefully. We can read many scenes as shooting scripts, complete with lighting, blocking, and direction. Even the illustrations, which Dickens supervised, resemble well-prepared storyboards, with engravings emphasizing action. If we see as Dickens wants us to see, I argue, then we will more quickly agree with what he has to tell us. (The same ploy can work in teaching nonfiction as well.)

Eisenstein's writing also proved helpful in discussing metaphor, since he describes montage, or associative cutting, as a visual trope. Metaphor is often a process of visualization, of attaching a physical image to an abstract idea. This notion helped complete the discussion of mixed metaphors and dying images raised by Orwell in "Politics and the English Language," and it encouraged students to risk new combinations in their writing.

Of course, I couldn't resist using the 1934 George Cukor film. Who can imagine Micawber as anyone but W. C. Fields (although Charles Laughton was producer David Selznick's first choice)? More than any other adaptation of a Dickens novel, the *David Copperfield* film presents characters precisely from the pages. But despite the perfect casting, the film exposes the novel's weaknesses (most prominently, its choppy, episodic structure) and points out the function of various characters and sequences that were left on the cutting room floor. We talked about other film adaptations and about what makes a film good.

When I realized that most of my students who didn't read a great deal call all essays "stories," I recognized that stories always hold their attention. If I offered them sustained reading pleasure and plenty of stories in one book, I reasoned, they would read more—and more carefully. At the end of the semester, I knew that they had completed and appreciated a major work of literature; for many, mine was the last English class they would ever take. I enjoyed teaching something I hold dear, and I know I taught better for it. Since composition courses dominate more and more teaching loads today, instructors need to find ways to use and share their literary training. Granted, not being able to examine Dickens in more detail frustrated me, but I knew that intensive literary treatment was not appropriate. The text did intimidate some weaker students, but the number who dropped didn't exceed the department average. I had not given my students a broad reading experience, but what they had read, they read closely.

Above all, *David Copperfield* helped me deal with a variety of problems rampant in the teaching of composition. These problems never seemed clearer than during a heated departmental debate over thesis statements and the emphasis on teaching what I saw as stilted, prefabricated organizational techniques. I argued that many essays we admire defy rules that we ask students to follow. "But we're not trying to teach our students how to write," a colleague tried to convince me; "we're teaching them how to write student essays." Most of my students are not planning careers writing "student essays." Who does? I want to help them confront any writing task, understand the process involved in producing effective prose, and sense the pleasure of fitting the word to the meaning. Sharing *David Copperfield* convinced many of them that the concerns of English teachers might have a place in their own lives.

Because I teach students who are often branded "nontraditional," I need to find nontraditional approaches. When I started teaching, this belief led me away from literary masterpieces in search of "relevant" readings, but finally I realized that hesitating to expose my students to great works revealed a prejudice. Instead of wondering whether they were good enough to tackle Dickens, I should have been asking myself whether Dickens could withstand their impatience and initial disapproval. Dickens' novels never seem stale to me; would the same hold true for my students? And what had I been protecting—my students or my precious idea of literature? Once I had taken the risk, I discovered that Dickens does still work, and that—not all the leather-bound volumes or critical texts or university courses—is what makes him a great writer.

David Copperfield: Parallel Reading for Undergraduates

J. Gill Holland

One of the chief delights of reading Dickens is to let the imagination go. In this paper I suggest a way of encouraging *David Copperfield* students to let their imaginations romp in the library amid the riches of Dickens material and at the same time—through the discipline of journal keeping and possibly a final research paper—to train their noses. Some teachers might say that parallel reading in contemporary material—letters, newspapers, or other fiction—or in modern critical and historical studies is far wide of the mark. Certainly the last thing desired is backsliding into the sins of the old dispensation, before New Criticism reminded us that the text is always paramount. We vow never again to neglect the work itself. Yet in reading Dickens we must not forget that much more than the naked work lies on the pages before us. The traditions behind the novel as a genre and the Victorian context in which the author set pen to paper both inform that work. Teachers should no more act as if *David Copperfield* existed in a vacuum than they should smother its glories under heaps of distracting outside material. We may not assume that students can frame the novel properly without help. As close as it may be in time, Dickens' world is not our own. Moreover, failure to push outward stunts the exploratory imagination. For Dickens, a well-exercised imagination meant fuller sympathy, with which came the giant step toward the betterment of our general lot. We will do greater violence to the expansive spirit of the master if we ignore the surrounding wealth of tradition and historical moment.

The swiftest way into the argument for parallel reading is to let an example speak for itself. Here are the final lines of a popular dramatization of the novel:

> **David:** Agnes!
> **Agnes:** Life, hope, and honor recovered! I am thine, thine forever! [*They embrace.*]
> **Heep:** Oh, no! This is a conspiracy! You have met here by appointment! You're a pretty set of people, ain't you, to buy over my clerk, who is the very scum of society; but I'll have some of you under the harrow! As for *you*, Micawber, I'll crush you yet! Give me that pocket-book—you had better! [*Micawber hits him with ruler.*]
> **Micawber:** Approach me again, and if your head is human, I'll break it, you heap of iniquity!
> **Heep:** Foiled!—Ruined!—Undermined! May the curses—
> **Micawber:** Ladies, sir, ladies! Respect feminine nerves, and retire decently to—in point of fact, jail! Who's swallowing swords now? [*Exit Heep and officers.*] (Brougham 23)

This climax can alert students to many delights and can lead them to consider the nature of literary appreciation. Melodrama has its own special rewards, and to look inside oneself after finishing such a piece is to perform a remarkable autopsy. Why is comedy often close to violence? Against what background of frightful possibilities does the author of melodrama play us for laughs? What is Gothic comedy, and how does conflict function in Gothic comedy? If pondered over and then given a paragraph or two in the reading log, these questions and others can lead to significant insights into both the play and the novel. Whether students muse alone or read the lines out loud with others, writing down reactions in a journal afterwards can help them savor Dickens' stories.

Before going further into the parallel reading journal, I should explain how I handle this novel in a course. I teach *David Copperfield* in "Victorian Literature" and in "English Fiction from Dickens." Both are electives pitched to juniors and seniors with varying backgrounds in literature; of the twenty-five to thirty students in an average class, a little over half are English majors. Out of a ten-week term I allow two weeks for the long Victorian novel of the course: *David Copperfield, Bleak House, The Woman in White, Daniel Deronda*, or some other substantial work. On the syllabus this novel is preceded by something short—such as *Three Men in a Boat, She, Dr. Jekyll and Mr. Hyde*, or (in the survey of Victorian literature) poetry—over which we can linger in discussion while the students read ahead into the three-decker. Dividing to conquer, a number of students will choose to specialize on this long work. They prepare a one-page class handout—on which they summarize plot briefly, note key scenes, list minor characters, and record the development of major characters—and finally offer the class their best critical insight into the narrative artistry of their section of the novel. *David Copperfield* breaks down easily into six handouts of two monthly numbers each beginning with number 7; the first six and final two numbers are not parceled out. The instructor leads the way through the first six parts; then, working in pairs, twelve students cover the next twelve, each pair beginning its discussion by reading through the handout quickly. (The remaining students in the class will have signed up to do the same for other long or difficult works to be read during the term.) The advantages of this division of labor are threefold: the students present a portion of the text that is manageable for upper-division majors and nonmajors; the class as a whole is eased into good discussion; and the instructor finds that this structure allows students to handle a giant novel in a survey course. By the time the last two numbers come up, everyone usually has respectable ideas about Dickens' artistry and can contribute to a final discussion of the novel.

Parallel reading complements this pedagogical treatment of the novel well. On the first day of class I explain what has already been set forth on the syllabus: a minimum of three hours' parallel reading in the library is required every week (this includes the time taken to write the entry), and a notebook is to be kept in which the student records date, time spent, and full bibliographical information for each work entry. The main body of the entry contains two things: basic information gleaned and a personal reaction to what has been read. The latter is important, for here students actively make connections with other readings. Periodically they should look back and assess earlier entries. Most students can tell useful notes from useless notes once they realize that they keep the notebook not simply to please the instructor but to record their own odyssey.

In asking for a journal of parallel reading from each student, the instructor must make a choice about the better way to teach: lead the way into the morass or let youth find its own way. I have found that, after the first few steps, it is better to point than to lead; there will be time to lead further when students have found topics for the research paper. In the light armor of the Clarendon *David Copperfield* (ed. Burgis), which is kept on reserve in the library, and Richard Dunn's *David Copperfield* bibliography, students can move fast, range widely, and find works they want to spend time on. Granted, there is more danger of wasted effort if the teacher does not help them over every obstacle, but the students gain more by working on their own. The instructor who provides long checklists of representative ancillary material is liable to smother the undergraduate. The object is love of learning, not love of a graduate-school ideal of thoroughness. Even assigning two thirds of the different approaches to *David Copperfield* would over-come students interested in the pleasures of reading Dickens rather than in a complete taxonomy of the subject. With Dunn's bibliography in hand, they will soon find something they want to pursue. Direct guidance would save minutes, but at what cost? The instructor's favorite topic of crime or social satire or whatever in Dickens, while worthy enough in itself, might shut off a young soul on its way to a personal *David Copperfield* in Tolstoy's youth (see Leavis and Leavis 35–36 and nn. 2, 3) or Dickens' own testimony in his letters that the novel is about himself: "I seem to be sending some part of myself into the shadowy world . . ." (*Selected Letters* 172). Or Henry James's embarrassment over the first-person point of view in *David Copperfield* might nag another student. A teacher should remember that what one finds, one owns, whether it be a treasure in Tolstoy or a quarrel in James. There is such a cornucopia of discoveries to be made about *David Copperfield* that it is folly to straitjacket the undergraduates who spend three hours a week in the library on their own. Let them find and treasure for themselves the dialogue from the discarded manuscript passage in which Steerforth first calls at Peggotty's boat, meets little Em'ly, and says to Mrs. Gummidge, "Come! Let us be lone and lorn together. Everything shall go contrairy with us both, and we'll go contrairy with all the world" (Burgis,

Clarendon ed., ch. 21). Ambling along byways of surprise has its Shandean rewards in Dickens library work.

This method leads naturally into the research paper called for at the end of the course. About halfway through the course the instructor or, preferably, a reference librarian leads a workshop in the reference section of the library. After several weeks of parallel reading, the students are ready to focus on an area of special interest in which to select a topic for concentrated investigation. At the beginning of the workshop they receive a single-sheet checklist of reference tools on which to record the steps of the search: national bibliographies (National Union Catalog, Bibliothèque Nationale, etc.), annual bibliographies (MLA, Humanities, IBZ, etc.), specialized bibliographies, dictionaries, book-review indexes, newspaper indexes, *DNB*, and so on. The librarian explains how these tools will help make exploration more efficient as students narrow their attention. At the end of this class-long workshop another librarian, in charge of interlibrary loans, explains briefly the network of borrowing in the United States and on the Solinet calls up and prints out the data for a title not in the school library holdings. This technological demonstration tops off the library period nicely. I might add that though the timing of the workshop might seem late, students are not nearly so interested in reference help for an assignment due months later as they are for a more imminent accounting; like the final examination it is an event that might not ever actually arrive.

The purpose in parallel reading is to amplify and discipline, to deepen students' understanding of *David Copperfield* and the larger world of Dickens, to lead the student toward maturity of thought through scrutiny and judgment in the notebook entries, and eventually—for those who elect to write the research paper on Dickens—to guide them to a worthwhile topic for final concentration. In the center is the novel itself, from which there are many paths. One can sort through the cutting-room floor and discover lost moments like Steerforth's conversation with Mrs. Gummidge. One can scan indexes to studies of later Dickens readers like James Joyce, who in *Ulysses* gently parodies the Pure-Faiths as Mrs. Purefoy calls in childbirth to her husband, "O Doady!" as though she were Dora calling David (420). Latter-day revisionists like Robert Graves send us back to the original words of the tale; Graves's esteem for stylistic economy so deludes him that he includes in an appendix a sample of Dickens' original so readers can agree on the alleged superiority of the rewrite for themselves. In studying Graves's approximations students uncover the old gold afresh. Or, if they prefer the rigors of a different mode of speculative thinking, they can apply Roman Jakobson's theory of metonymy and realism to the Dickensian prose of *David Copperfield* (see Romano).

Circling out from the text at the center, the student finds in every ring further opportunity for exploration and critical contemplation. What

Dickens felt about the post office, the Great Exhibition, forgeries, slums, insane asylums, arctic exploration, and the London Foundling Hospital ("Received, a Blank Child") can be appreciated in selections from *Household Words*, a journal that came into being after the initially slow sales of *David Copperfield* revealed that contemporary fans wanted their comic and not our later, darker Dickens (see Harry Stone, *Uncollected Writings*, and Ganz 23–24). As the story of Dickens' personal life draws us in, the plethora of uneven biographical sleuthing tests our sympathies and demands judgment. Salvos over Dickens' private life will continue to be exchanged for years to come. There is no better way for students to temper their credulity before the printed word than to read a bit about Dickens and Ellen Ternan (Wagenknecht 11–40; see also *Dickens and the Scandalmongers*, Rev. of; Minerof; and "Charles and Ellen"). Who does not learn something about the lines between dream, reality, and art from the Maria Beadnell contretemps, when the childhood vision of the original Dora turned to ashes? "The star of his own life from boyhood [became], in a moment, putrid vapour" (Stonehouse xii), and the ironic melodramatist was left with his just deserts, a case of the common cold (Dickens, *Selected Letters* 159). Out of all of this—history, biography, criticism—students can find a storehouse to explore and ponder. They might eventually discover that Dickens has shaped visions all over the world. Dostoevsky read *David Copperfield* in Siberia; Kafka read it in Prague; Lao She wanted to write about Peking the way Dickens wrote about London (Churchill 141; Dunn, *Bibliography* xxiii; Jean James vii, ix). A stronger, clearer imagination rewards the reader who looks out over David's Kentish seashore through the eyes of the future George Eliot or sees the Victorian tableaux of *David Copperfield* as its famous illustrators did or along the sights of film directors like Sergei Eisenstein (Haight 113–14; Cohen 100–07; Eisenstein 195–234; Ortman 115–30).

The possibilities for critical exploration go on and on. The Dickens bibliographies, companions, annuals, symposia, encyclopedias, journals, newsletters, readers, digests, clubs, fellowships, and centenaries will never stop, and the student should not fear them.

Multum in Parvo: The Ninth Chapter of David Copperfield

George J. Worth

As everyone who teaches long Victorian novels knows, it is extremely difficult to grasp one of those "loose, baggy monsters" firmly enough to gain any precise sense of how the author has deployed the multitude of characters, incidents, themes, and techniques with which he or she dazzles the reader. If we find it hard to reduce (and I am mindful of the pejorative connotations of the word) such a complex text to any kind of order, the task must seem overwhelming to our students—even, perhaps especially, to the best of them. But once we acknowledge that we cannot hold a nine-hundred-page novel in our minds the way we can a sonnet—and thus cannot readily analyze all its parts, their interconnections, and their relations to a clearly perceived whole—the question arises, How do we deal with a work like *David Copperfield* without either taking refuge in grand and vague generalizations or else pointing fatuously to the numerous "beauties" and also the occasional "blemishes" that Dickens has produced? (I am assuming that no class of undergraduates will sit still for any attempt to deconstruct the novel.)

One place to begin is with the recognition that even readers of limited experience and sophistication, such as most undergraduates, can achieve at least a rough-and-ready sense of the "whole" of such a work with enough time and proper guidance. Assuming that one cannot speak intelligently about a piece of literature unless one has read it in its entirety, I normally give my students in a course on Dickens or on the nineteenth-century British novel a couple of weeks at the beginning of the term to read the first text while I lecture or dismiss class; then, while we discuss it, they read the second; and so on. To direct their attention to some major issues that we shall consider together, I provide them with a set of eight to twelve study questions for each novel before they begin reading. This arrangement is in many ways artificial and unsatisfactory, but there is bound to be something artificial and unsatisfactory about reading and discussing such a work as part of a syllabus and under academic pressures rather than at leisure over, say, nineteen months as the separate numbers come out. It goes without saying that a student will spend far more time reading *David Copperfield* than talking or writing about it and that, given the other demands of the usual formal course, much in a novel of this length and complexity will be neither discussed nor written about. Perhaps we should remind ourselves that, unlike some contemporary novels, *David Copperfield* was written to be enjoyed rather than to be taught: teaching it as we wish to and must will inevitably entail some compromises.

Though anything but simple, ordering our perceptions of a long and complicated novel is easier in the case of *David Copperfield*, narrated by the protagonist throughout, than in that of its immediate successor in the Dickens canon, *Bleak House,* where the clashing voices of Esther Summerson and the unnamed disembodied narrator are constantly played off against each other. For David remains David: though the character develops as he grows up, the mature narrator is looking back on his "personal history" after the substantial portion of it that goes into the plot is over; he can judge what happens to him in the light of later knowledge, though of course he may choose for reasons of his own to withhold such judgment. Obviously his voice is anything but monotone; on the contrary, it expresses different moods, takes on different inflections. But it is always unmistakably David's, and its distinctiveness does much to hold the novel together.

Another feature of *David Copperfield* can also help us discover some kind of organizing principle in it. As Jerome H. Buckley has pointed out, the novel is the protagonist's "autobiography as the product of a powerful memory working over his experience from childhood to early maturity" (35). David is a highly self-conscious author, and so this "autobiography" is largely made up not of an undifferentiated flow of events but rather of carefully selected, intensely felt, and vividly remembered episodes in his life—Wordsworthian "spots of time." Almost everywhere one looks in *David Copperfield,* one can find in such episodes characteristics and significances that resonate throughout the novel.

Any consideration of *David Copperfield* based on a reading of the whole novel is bound to lead to some general notions about it. If what I have said so far is valid, it should be possible to test, refine, and extend these insights by examining the narrative voice and the autobiographical memory as they work together in a single episode or chapter. Such technical characteristics will be significant and effective locally, but they will also serve to remind readers of what happens elsewhere in the text, thus strengthening their sense of its unity. I would also argue, though I shall not be able to prove this point here, that the more episodes or chapters—preferably varying in subject matter and occurring in different parts of the novel—one inspects in this way, the surer one's sense of *David Copperfield* as a coherent work of art will become.

For purposes of this essay, I have chosen to look at chapter 9, "I Have a Memorable Birthday." The title refers to the fact that, after returning to Salem House Academy for his second half-year, David receives the news of his mother's death on what is presumably his ninth birthday. (In chapter 5, on his way to school for the first time, David told the rascally waiter in the inn at Yarmouth that he was "between eight and nine.") He goes home for the funeral; that evening Peggotty tells him the story of his mother's decline and final fatal illness. And so the chapter ends—hardly the most eventful of the sixty-four in the novel, yet full of interest for those who wish to come to terms with *David Copperfield.*

David starts the chapter by remarking that though he had been back at school a "full two months" before that "memorable birthday," he can "remember nothing" of the "gap" between January and March. "The great remembrance by which that time is marked in my mind, seems to have swallowed up all lesser recollections, and to exist alone." David's memory works selectively, here and everywhere in the novel. When it is operating, however, it is uncanny in its seemingly total recall both of the often complicated, sometimes synesthetic sensory impressions that impinge on him and of his own reactions to what befalls him. There are several particularly striking examples in this chapter, each of which will richly repay whatever attention readers are induced to bring to it.

The third paragraph begins, "How well I recollect the kind of day it was!" It continues, like the four "retrospective" chapters (18, 43, 53, and 64) and the other accounts of especially distinct memories, in the present tense, switching from the past of *was*, and for good reason: as David says before the great storm in chapter 55 (which is, however, narrated in the past tense), "I do not recall it, but see it done; for it happens again before me." In chapter 9, David *smells* "the fog that hung about" Salem House, *sees* "the hoar frost, ghostly, through it," *feels* his "rimy hair fall clammy" on his cheek, and employs several senses simultaneously as he perceives "the dim perspective of the schoolroom, with a sputtering candle here and there to light up the foggy morning, and the breath of the boys wreathing and smoking in the raw cold as they blow upon their fingers, and tap their feet upon the floor."

When David is summoned to the Creakles' parlor after breakfast, he thinks, mistakenly, that a birthday hamper from Peggotty has arrived. He provides a tableau, no less vivid for its terseness, of what he sees on entering the room: "Mr. Creakle, sitting at his breakfast with the cane and a newspaper before him, and Mrs. Creakle with an opened letter in her hand. But no hamper." The headmaster's wife tells David about his mother's death as kindly as she can, and he gives way to his emotion only gradually: "A mist rose between Mrs. Creakle and me, and her figure seemed to move in it for an instant. Then I felt the burning tears run down my face, and it was steady again." David does finally break down and cry, but it is not primarily on his grief that his memory and narrative focus. He "began to think" after he "could cry no more," and prominent in his thoughts are what Dickens in his notes for the third monthly number of *David Copperfield* called "childish incidental whimsicalities" (Butt and Tillotson 123): David peeks into a mirror "to see how red my eyes were, and how sorrowful my face"; he worries about the possibility that he might commit an impropriety by not weeping at the funeral and ponders what "it would affect me most to think of when I drew near home" in order to make the tears flow again; his bereavement gives him a new sense of self-importance, and he strikes "melancholy" attitudes as he walks "in the playground that afternoon while the boys were in school," aware that they are looking at him "out of the windows." David the narrator is not minimizing his own grief; rather, as he does on innumerable occasions, he deliberately qualifies with other emotions the pity the reader is likely to feel for him. Its mixture of pathos and comedy makes the passage useful for comparison with, for example, the conversation between David and Mr. Barkis near the opening of chapter 5.

As a boy David seems fated to confront strangers at the end of anxious journeys, when the sight of a familiar face would be especially reassuring. Just as he was collected by Mr. Mell after he arrived at the "Blue Something" in Whitechapel (ch. 5), so now Mr. Omer meets his coach in Yarmouth. This "fat, short-winded, merry-looking, little old man in black, with rusty little bunches of ribbons at the knees of his breeches, black stockings, and a broad-brimmed hat" takes David to his place of business, that of a "DRAPER, TAILOR, HABERDASHER, FUNERAL FURNISHER, &c," catering to the living and the dead alike. Throughout his stay in Mr. Omer's shop, where "there was a good fire . . . and a breathless smell of warm black crape—I did not know what the smell was then, but I know now," and the journey back home to Blunderstone in Mr. Omer's chaise, David is reminded again and again of a fact that has been dawning on him throughout the chapter, though his narrative never dwells on it: the close proximity of life and death in his world. Indeed this fact permeates the entire novel, beginning on the first page, where we learn that David came into that world shrouded in a caul, supposed to be a talisman against drowning. Later in the first chapter we learn that he was "a posthumous child": his father remains something of a presence in the nearby churchyard, but his absence in life has a profound effect on David's history. The delightful home of Mr. Peggotty to which David was introduced in chapter 3 is populated by the survivors of "drowndead" fishermen. *David Copperfield* contains its appropriate Dickensian quota of deaths; at least three of these—Ham's, Steerforth's, and Mr. Spenlow's—are sudden and unexpected. In chapter 9, Mr. Omer constantly muses on this subject of death-in-life. While he is preparing to measure David for his mourning suit, the boy keeps hearing the "RAT-tat-tat, RAT-tat-tat, RAT-tat-tat" of one of Mr. Omer's employees pounding away on his mother's coffin. When the carpenter, Joram, comes in, he flirts with Mr. Omer's daughter Minnie in front of David, whose mind is "running on very different things." In the chaise—actually, as David describes it in his customary fidelity to detail, "a kind of half chaise-cart, half pianoforte-van, painted of a sombre colour, and drawn by a black horse with a long tail"—the Omers and Joram maintain their cheerful demeanor. "I do not think," David remarks, "I have ever experienced so strange a feeling in my life (I am wiser now, perhaps) as that of being with them, remembering how they had been employed, and seeing them enjoy the ride."

For his account of the funeral, David returns to the present tense, thus signaling this scene's climactic significance in the chapter. Once again David's senses, and his memory of what they enabled him to perceive, are at full stretch:

> If the funeral had been yesterday, I could not recall it better. The very air of the best parlour, when I went in at the door, the bright condition of the fire, the shining of the wine in the decanters, the patterns of the glasses and plates, the faint sweet smell of cake, the odour of Miss Murdstone's dress, and our black clothes.

"I remark everything," he comments. When the funeral is over, he says of it, as he might have said of other key episodes in the novel: "All this . . . is yesterday's event. Events of later date have floated from me to the shore where all forgotten things will reappear [an image of the afterlife familiar to those who have read Dickens' preceding novel, *Dombey and Son*], but this stands like a high rock in the ocean." One might add that David's is not the only memory that comes into play here: for the reader as well, the little procession to the churchyard, the graveside service, the return to the Rookery, and David's emotions during these sad events, as precisely rendered as they are, are as close to being unforgettable as anything in prose fiction can be. In recounting them, David denies that "I care about myself, or have done since I came home," adding that, despite his preternatural awareness of what is going on around him, "I mind nothing but my grief." An attempt to reconcile these apparently contradictory statements with each other and with Sylvère Monod's reference to David's "pronounced self-centeredness" (317) will yield considerable insight into the narrative method of *David Copperfield*.

Chapter 9 ends with the conversation between Peggotty and David during which she tells him the circumstances of his mother's death, followed by two paragraphs in which David reflects on the meaning to him of everything that has happened since he awoke on the morning of his "memorable birthday." As I have argued elsewhere, Peggotty's story, placed where it is, is deliberately anticlimactic (Worth 104). Because David already knows the outcome, because he has already had ample opportunity to purge himself of his grief, and because he hears of Clara's last moments from someone else instead of being present at her passing, this dialogue is surprisingly free of pathos. Especially since Dickens is sometimes reviled for his handling of deathbed scenes, it is interesting to note that David witnesses only one in the course of this long novel: that of a minor character,

Mr. Barkis (ch. 30). Just as David was absent when his mother died, so he later misses the even more important death of Dora (ch. 53). Again the pathos is muted: the narrator deflects the reader's attention from the dying young woman to her remorseful husband, berating himself for his "undisciplined heart."

The closing paragraphs bring up once again the theme of death-in-life, but with a difference. David cannot think of the body in the newly filled grave as that of a woman wasted by illness; to him she is "the young mother of my earliest impressions, who had been used to wind her bright curls round and round her finger, and to dance with me at twilight in the parlour." If this represents life-in-death rather than death-in-life, then David's thought of his infant half-brother, buried with Clara, suggests the reverse: "the little creature in her arms, was myself, as I had once been, hushed for ever on her bosom." Though a nine-year-old boy by the name of David Copperfield continues to live, the dependent child who once bore that name is now irretrievably gone. A new David—alone in the world, deprived not only of his mother but also of his old nurse when Peggotty marries Barkis in the next chapter—is about to set out on a series of grim adventures in London and on a nightmare journey to Dover before attaining a new kind of dependency with Betsey Trotwood in chapter 14.

David's memories and his strategies for dealing with them in narrative are by no means the only features of chapter 9 that connect it with the rest of the novel. When Jane Murdstone speaks to David "in an iron whisper," the reader recalls the imagery associated with that "metallic lady" during her introduction in chapter 4 and elsewhere; renewed mention of her "firmness" here is part of a plan to inject into *David Copperfield* the theme of self-discipline, on which Dickens later plays so many variations. Her brother Edward, however, appears in this chapter in a new light: grief-stricken in his bereavement, he sits "by the fireside, weeping silently, and pondering in his elbow-chair," when David comes home for the funeral. Could it be that David was not entirely right in his earlier condemnation of Murdstone, that Clara was not entirely wrong in entering on her second marriage? The foreshadowings in chapter 9 range from the obvious (David's comment on leaving Salem House that "I little thought then that I left it, never to return") to the subtle (do we remember Peggotty's avowal that "she never would desert" David's mother when Mrs. Micawber begins declaiming three chapters later that "I will never desert Mr. Micawber"?).

I would contend, then, that a class period devoted to a close reading of a single chapter of *David Copperfield*, such as chapter 9, will "open up" the novel in many useful ways, provided that (a) students have already gained a sense of the whole from one complete reading and (b) the chapter is approached as part of that whole and not merely as a self-contained entity. This kind of analysis, of course, has other pedagogical virtues in an age when the reading comprehension and the general knowledge of our students leave much to be desired, but that is a subject for another and more overtly polemical essay.

The procedure I have sketched can apply—with appropriate modifications—to virtually any chapter of *David Copperfield*. I have had some success with the "retrospective" chapters and chapters 2 and 45; other attractive candidates are chapters 16, 22, 36, 44, and 58. Because both class time and students' patience are finite, teachers should probably limit themselves to examining four or five chapters in this way before finishing (rather than simply abandoning) the novel by attempting to formulate some general statements about it. These may deal with the narrative voice, the function of memory, or any other major issues the class has identified together. What I am advocating is not as simple as an inductive movement from the particular to the general, because individual chapters will not make much sense without at least a preliminary grasp of the whole novel and also because general statements are meaningless unless they can be related to particular evidence. Rather, I have tried to suggest how initial hypotheses about *David Copperfield* may be turned into defensible propositions by means that will enhance our students' enjoyment along with their understanding.

Testing by Installments the "Undisciplined Heart" of *David Copperfield*'s Reader

Michael Lund

A familiar difficulty in teaching masterpieces of literature, particularly to undergraduates, is that many students are too young to appreciate some of the ideas that interest older writers, critics, and teachers. While prodigies may master calculus at the age of eight, it is the other way around in literature, where the more mature student brings to class an enthusiasm deriving from personal experience. Both the form and the content of *David Copperfield*—and, in fact, of many other Victorian novels—make this traditional problem of a lack of experience less severe. Not only does *Copperfield* treat questions of maturity as subject matter (as do many other works of fiction in the nineteenth century), its form insists on maturity from its reader.

David Bleich argues in *Subjective Criticism* that "each person's most urgent motivations are to understand himself . . . " (297). Further, he claims, "the interpretation of an aesthetic object is motivated . . . by the desire to create knowledge on one's own behalf and on behalf of one's community from the subjective experience of the work of art" (93). In relation to *David Copperfield*, as it is read and taught in the classroom, Bleich's assertions suggest that a group of twenty-year-old collegians will be in search of an understanding particular to their stage in life, something discernibly different from what is sought by a night class of older adults returning to school after some years. They will not (necessarily) read different texts, but they will be more likely to notice, and attribute meaning to, those parts of the text that answer their special desires.

The process of growth, for example—striving to achieve adult status in emotional relationships and in vocation—is an aspect of *David Copperfield* as bildungsroman that particularly interests typical undergraduates. In my classes, many students seem to home in on the central character's effort to grow up into a responsible, respected adult, reflecting, of course, their own desire at this crucial stage of their development. One of my recent students most taken with *Copperfield*, for instance, wrote a paper on "the development of David's character through a pattern of conflict and resolution." Another considered the issue of growth manifested in Micawber, whose history shows that "he is always trying to establish himself in society." Many students follow the women characters' development which, one comments, is always "restrained" by their environment. Another student shrewdly observes that Emily "leaps at the chance of bettering herself" through her relationship to Steerforth. And one student even explored the ways in which "sea imagery [conveys] David's movement through life." Recognizing the central theme (the protagonist's evolving maturity) and the serial structure of *Copperfield*, a teacher can take advantage of student-readers' interest in growth and encourage them in their own desire to achieve adulthood. The reader's "undisciplined heart" can be a tool in the teacher's effort to conduct a class, just as David Copperfield's "undisciplined heart" is a key to Dickens' success in creating a novel about the maturing of the protagonist. As one of my best students wrote, Dickens' skills "allow the reader to actually participate in the experiences which parallel the nature of David's own."

That the protagonist's movement toward maturity is the novel's central subject needs no extended argument here; many critics have traced in detail the pattern of David's gradual recognition that "my own heart was undisciplined" (ch. 48). That the reader's heart might change, however, and that this change is a central part of the literary experience of *David Copperfield*, requires further explanation. This notion is easier to accept when one considers the novel's original nineteen-month serialization. Literary scholarship has already documented that this serial context can change the text. Miss Mowcher, who first appears in the novel's eighth number (Dec. 1849), alters in character by the time of her second appearance, in number 11 (March 1850), because Mrs. Seymour Hill wrote to Dickens claiming that the fictional portrait resembled, and thus ridiculed, her. Following his audience's desire, Dickens allowed his conception of the fictional world to alter in time; it may be that readers' conceptions of the fictional world also change as they move through the novel and as their own relations to their (real) worlds develop.

To recognize and use this change in the classroom or to measure its exact shape, however, we need to emphasize the fiction's temporal framework by teaching the novel in installments, returning the student to the mode in which it was first read and through which it first made itself a force in our culture (for a list of installment numbers and corresponding chapter numbers, see Appendix). Of course, the regular academic semester or quarter does not allow for an exact reproduction of the original reading timetable. Instead of the year and a half or more that Victorians took to complete the novel, our students will generally have about four months. Either of two approaches remains open, however: teaching one installment at a time on a regular schedule (almost every class) throughout the entire term or doubling up, teaching two or three of the original installments at a time, each assignment coming about a week or ten days apart. Sometimes the suspense of a particular cliff-hanger is lessened if one's syllabus requires lumping several parts together, but this second approach still features the lengthened experience and the recognition that there are gaps in the reading prpocess. I have found doubling up easier, perhaps because some other important installment novels (*Middlemarch, Anna Karenina, The Prime Minister*) come in eight parts, each about two or three times as long as a Dickens monthly number; and I prefer to allow as much time between installments as possible for students to add to their understanding of the fictional situations. (One does not, of course, have to devote an entire class to discussion of the installment novel. In fact, one often finds that discussion of one aspect of the serial novel leads to a larger discussion involving other works in the course.)

The type of course will frequently suggest a schedule. For a class in the British novel, primarily made up of English majors, more space between installments of the featured long novel seems advisable, since between readings in the long novel comes consideration of other complete works like *Robinson Crusoe, Pride and Prejudice,* and *Wuthering Heights.* In a sophomore-level survey course in British or Western literature, taken by many nonmajors, scheduling shorter, more frequent readings in the featured long novel keeps the students familiar with the plot and gives them detailed knowledge of one central literary work, to which they can relate other works, as well as considerations of literary history.

Teaching in installments has additional advantages: for many of today's undergraduates, less familiar with literature and less able to handle long novels than earlier generations of students were, reading one or two installments at a time is simply easier. Discussing smaller sections of the text in several classes at least a week apart also ensures a fuller, closer knowledge of the total novel. And this approach encourages teachers to reexperience the novel along with their students and, generally, to foster more (and more open) discussion in the classroom instead of simply presenting again the set of notes worked up in the past.

In addition to these benefits of installment teaching, which accrue to any novel, *David Copperfield* particularly grants to students and teacher another range of opportunity. The serial structure of *David Copperfield* reinforces the stages of the protagonist's growth and encourages the reader's recognition that such development is often painfully slow, unsteady, even frustrating, but that growth is, in the end, always possible. This discovery helps convince students of something they often have not had time to realize in their own lives: that the development of a mature self is a long-term, gradual process. Business administration majors just entering college usually picture the first job after graduation as a challenging managerial position in which their unique talents will be turned loose to solve problems unencountered by earlier generations. Our own English majors, often imagining themselves future writers, are not any more ready to acknowledge that the production of great literature requires years of hard work. Struggling with a long novel over an entire semester often impresses on the survivors an understanding that mastery of a skill or subject involves more time and effort than they had originally thought. (And even those who fall off the wagon of weekly reading assignments learn from seeing the competence of others that diligence pays off—it is seldom in our profession that failure is so productive!)

We can see the novel's structural pattern, which underscores this difficulty of accomplishment and the simple time necessary in growing up, by considering the conclusions of the monthly numbers, where David's position on the way to adulthood is dramatically and regularly stressed. While teaching in parts gives additional emphasis to other aspects of this great novel, the conclusions of individual installments—simply because they linger in the reader's consciousness while he or she is between parts—are perhaps the most convenient place to look for evidence that the serial structure helps create meaning. Written assignments done outside class as the reading continues can often ensure the students' awareness of important biographical and historical contexts; but class time almost inevitably is taken up with the crucial moment of each installment, its conclusion.

In the first four installment endings, for example, the protagonist's littleness at the beginning of his journey through life is emphasized by comparisions to others. At the end of number 1, a small David cowers before "a great dog—deep-mouthed and black-haired like Him [Murdstone]" (ch. 3). Number 2 concludes as David compares himself to "a person of great power" (ch. 6), Steerforth, whose stature at Salem House sets off the hero's insignificance. His mother's death, at the end of number 3, reiterates the theme of David's threatened identity. With his sense of himself almost extinguished by this loss, David sees in the image of the dead Mrs. Murdstone "the mother of my infancy" and in that of his dead brother "myself, as I had once been, hushed for ever on her bosom" (ch. 9). And running away from London at the end of part 4, David is diminished by a "long-legged young man" (ch. 12) who takes his money and his box with ease. (My student studying sea imagery noted that David had been "'set adrift' as a young boy in London" near the end of this installment.) All these striking images at the conclusions of individual installments stress that, in the eyes of the world, David Copperfield has barely begun his development as an individual. Almost any division of the novel into installments for a class will place one of these images in the student's mind, where it hovers for several weeks in the time between assignments, insisting on a central aspect of the novel's meaning—Copperfield as protagonist is moving slowly, if at all, toward his maturity. One veteran of my British novel class says, "The cycle of anticipatory hope and ensuing despair forms one of the major movements of the novel."

The second group of four installments contains endings with slightly more positive signs—David showing growth—but even here comparisons to other characters continue to reinforce the fact that the protagonist has more experience to undergo before he can reach maturity. At the end of number 5 the young David is safely adopted by his Aunt Betsey and housed at Wickfield's school, where he is "feeling friendly towards everybody"; yet he is apprehensive about the older and strangely knowledgeable Heep, wanting to "shut him out [of the house] in a hurry" (ch. 15). At the conclusion of number 6 an adolescent David "gloriously" defeats the butcher in a fistfight but is defeated himself by the angelic Miss Larkins (ch. 18). Number 7 ends contrasting David's innocence with Steerforth's worldliness as they visit Yarmouth together. Both are young men of some means and education, but the more trusting Copperfield fails to see in Steerforth anything except qualities to "admire and love" (ch. 21). And the novel's eighth number finishes with David's drunken dinner party in London, at which Agnes unexpectedly arrives. David is aware that her influence in his life "had so far improved me [that] I felt ashamed" but not enough that he possesses genuine maturity (ch. 24). Once again, reading the novel in installments puts before the students, for an extended period of contemplation as they await the continuation of Copperfield's adventures, a crucial scene in which the protagonist's growth is still limited. One student stresses this lack of mature judgment when she says that Copperfield "warms up to everyone, and stays vulnerable to everything until he also begins to learn...."

At this point in the novel the class is about one third of the way through the semester, and, in addition to learning that a character's development toward adulthood can be much slower than anticipated, students are beginning to realize that holding the pieces of a long, involved novel together in their heads over an extended time requires effort (maturity) on their own part. They do have some experience, of course: most of them have followed *General Hospital* or some other television soap opera through a summer at least, and one can always confront them with that kind of evidence of their skill. By now the discipline of reading regularly is being rewarded in class, because those who have kept up find that they have plenty to say about the next installment of *Copperfield* and that their insights clearly derive from detailed knowledge of earlier installments. Thus, while the course and the novel are hardly over, students have already had a number of opportunities to learn.

I find the next three installments of *David Copperfield* concluding in a new manner for the novel: David sees others in trouble at the ends of numbers 9, 10, and 11. Micawber, "fallen back, *for* a spring," is featured on the last page of number 9 (ch. 27). Commenting on this scene, one student points out that "David has to become a father figure to keep Micawber's affairs in order." Mr. Peggotty's sorrow at Emily's having run away with Steerforth dramatically affects David at the end of number 10. David, according to one student, feels "overcome with guilt and emotion" at "the desolation I had caused ... " (ch. 31). And the eleventh number finishes with Aunt Betsey Trotwood's announcement that she is "ruined" (ch. 34). Staggered by her loss, David is also impressed by Aunt Betsey's courage, her intention to "live misfortune down" (ch. 34). As one student writes, "David must now mature in order to resolve this new obstacle which has disrupted his life." This group of endings suggests that the protagonist is finally approaching a new maturity as the narrative of his life focuses on the troubles of others and on his responsibility to help them. Students find they are reading a novel in which the central character not only turns out "to be the hero of my own life" (ch. 1) but also is called on to assist others by his heroism.

The final scenes of the next three installments, however, return to the mode of the novel's first four: David's very identity as an individual is threatened. Number 12 concludes with David in love, surrounded by such a "forest of difficulty" in attempting to support a family that "I used to fancy that my head was turning quite grey" (ch. 37). (One student comments that "the task [of earning money] is not an easy one and takes much patience and perseverance, but in the end David masters the shorthand which helps prepare him later for his success as a writer.") As the parallel story of Emily's fall continues, number 13 concludes with an image of David's own possible disappearance: watching the sad figure of Mr. Peggotty walking into the distance, David observes that "my new track was the only one to be seen [in the snow]; and even that began to die away (it snowed so fast) as I looked back over my shoulder" (ch. 40). The conclusion to number 14 is David's marriage to Dora, but an older narrator looking back on the scene undercuts the sense of maturity one would attribute to the protagonists at such a moment: "I have stood aside to see the phantoms of those days go by me. They are gone, and I resume the journey of my story" (ch. 43). A class left with one or more of these images, after half the semester has passed, wonders if the novel's hero can ever escape the forces that seem to want to deny his existence.

The conclusions to the next four installments (after which comes only the novel's final double number) show David still uncertain about his role in society and his own identity, even though Dickens' audience knows the novel is drawing to a close. Number 15 concludes with David and Mr. Peggotty about to speak with Martha. David leads the way with a firm assertion, "We may speak to her now" (ch. 46). However, the final scene in number 16 shows David more as a passive onlooker; Emily, verbally assaulted by Rosa Dartle, collapses, to be rescued in a moment by her uncle. Although Copperfield could have stopped Rosa's attack, he chose not to, thinking: "I did not know what to do. Much as I desired to put an end to the interview, I felt that I had no right to present myself; that it was for Mr. Peggotty alone to see her and recover her" (ch. 50). Dora's death completes installment 17, and once again the protagonist's sense of himself seems absolutely overcome: "Darkness comes before my eyes; and, for a time, all things are blotted out of my remembrance" (ch. 53). (My sea-imagery student connects David's "inner turmoil" with a "rising sea of memory.") Number 18 resolves the difficulties of many of David's friends, as the company departs for Australia, but he remains behind, alone and uncertain: "The night had fallen on the Kentish hills when we were rowed ashore—and fallen darkly upon me" (ch. 57). At the last break between installments, then (as only the final double number remains to be read), Dickens' readers are left with a familiar image—a self that is painfuly, slowly emerging. The protagonist we have listened to and watched for eighteen months (or the length of an academic semester) has progressed in a number of key ways. He has grown older, escaped the domination of others who would have harmed him, and established himself in an independent profession, but he has failed to resolve the inner doubts about his own worth and values. Young students at the end of their long journey reading *David Copperfield* in parts have come to expect such uncertainty, such gradual but not necessarily inevitable movement toward a resolution. Although they may not make the connection to their own lives—realizing that they too are moving slowly toward a still distant maturity—teaching in installments encourages that kind of learning. One student, for instance, wrote that "The reader, too, becomes educated about human nature as Dickens allows him to view the gradual development of various characters in the novel."

Of course, there is evidence all along in the reading of *David Copperfield* that David will achieve maturity: the narrative voice of the novel is that of a mature adult looking back on the road he has traveled. Such assurance belongs in the nineteenth century, where the presence of so many bildungsromans reminds us of how important the notion of personal progress was for the age. Just as England and the civilization it represented were surely moving toward a more nearly perfect state, so individuals knew they could achieve significant places and functions in the social order. We should not, however, overemphasize this ultimate happy ending; the novel, after all, has already confronted us with eighteen unhappy ones. Modern criticism declares that the authors' desire to please their audiences by leaving characters married and prosperous at the end flawed the realism of Victorian fiction, but we must remember that for these characters success was always long in coming. Teaching long novels in installments brings back this often ignored characteristic of nineteenth-century fiction. One of my students who has read in parts and is close to articulating the complexity of growth in *David Copperfield* says, "The reader must also overcome the struggles in David's life and be prepared for the maturing that has taken place in David's character between publications [of the separate parts]."

In our own age, the assumption that a character can achieve anything is hardly automatic. Students in many literature courses are confronted with twentieth-century alienation and encouraged to suspect that the identity any fictional (or real) character constructs is an illusion, a momentary creation doomed to inevitable deconstruction. In *Lord Jim*, for example,

Jim's conviction that he has missed his one chance to achieve an identity worthy of his dreams is characteristic of the modern protagonist. Even though Conrad's classic was also serialized (*Blackwood's*, Oct. 1899 to Nov. 1900), its twentieth-century form contradicts the fundamental values of the bildungsroman. In teaching *David Copperfield* (and other Victorian classics) in installments, we are not only continuing to bring a masterpiece of literature to new generations of students; we are also affirming for the future a belief in the possibility of human achievement.

Teaching *David Copperfield*: Language, Psychoanalysis, and Feminism

Dianne F. Sadoff

Most contemporary criticism reminds us that, no matter how we think about texts, our insights are tempered by our blindness. All strategies for approaching narrative necessarily circumscribe our ability to perceive information that lies outside our methodology; all enabling assumptions about literature generate limitations. As critics and as teachers, we must call attention to such assumptions and limitations in our critical approaches, must question our set responses and our desire to master texts. Our students need to know our pedagogical and theoretical commitments, to feel they may view such perspectives as authoritative and earned by experience, but also to feel they may challenge these commitments and the readings a theory generates. Such authentic exchange in and out of the classroom keeps us fresh in our knowledge of literature and sharpens our pedagogical skills. It prevents us, I hope, from viewing students as folks who butter us up, rip us off for grades, plagiarize behind our backs, and desire only to learn our pedagogical secrets so as to puncture our fragile fictions of authority. My own commitments as teacher and critic might loosely be termed psychoanalytic, poststructuralist, and feminist; these commitments certainly affect the ways I teach literature and will also delimit this essay.

I have taught *David Copperfield* in a seminar for undergraduate English majors and nonmajors at the junior and senior levels. My students usually have little literary background but great sophistication about issues and values; they quickly learn my concern with language and metaphor. The course currently includes *Pride and Prejudice, Jane Eyre, Vanity Fair, Middlemarch,* and *Tess of the d'Urbervilles. David Copperfield* stands midway in the semester and represents "high Victorian" values as compared to turn-of-the-century rationalism, Romanticism, satire and skepticism, organic realism, and end-of-the-century nihilism. I find it most difficult to make my students see *David Copperfield*'s place in this picture of changing nineteenth-century values: they find David's obsessions with earnestness, punctuality, and duty less interesting than, for example, the novel's issues about sexuality and the family. The format of this class is primarily discussion-oriented; I will talk a good deal if inspired to do so and will bring background material to the students' reading of Dickens, but I do not lecture as such. My own beliefs about teaching assume that students must actively participate in their learning by formulating and testing ideas verbally in class, that groups work well together only when a high level of trust permits and encourages such risk taking, and that authentic learning requires human interaction. I expect to teach my students a skill—how to read a nineteenth-century novel in terms of its various contexts—rather than a set of facts about literature and social history.

My expectations of students' achievement in this class are both rigorous and informal. I have found the old New Critical approach to assigning reading in fiction classes—and particularly in Victorian fiction—unworkable. I allot five or six two-hour classes (two and a half or three weeks) to *David Copperfield* (as to *Middlemarch* and *Vanity Fair*) and ask students to read about twenty percent of the novel for each class. We do not, then, talk about the entire novel from the first day of our work with Dickens; rather, we work through the narrative, talking about issues as they arise and about the expectations they generate in us as we approach the next section of the novel. Reading Victorian fiction seems less formidable to students if approached this way, although a triple-decker frightens students even when assigned in pieces. I often choose, with such a lengthy narrative, to give my students a "reading day" in lieu of one class; *Copperfield*, however, tends to interest students sufficiently to keep them up-to-date in their reading—unlike *Vanity Fair* and *Middlemarch*. If students do fall behind or find interpreting so long a novel difficult, I provide study questions that focus their responses to the reading for the next class. I require class attendance and participation in discussion and consider both in my evaluation of a student's performance.

For *Copperfield*, I assign as reserve reading the autobiographical fragment, so students will understand the concept of fictional autobiography (John Forster 24-36). At the beginning of the semester, I hand out lists of recommended reading in literary criticism that my students occasionally use when writing papers about Dickens. I include on that list (in addition to traditional books on Victorian fiction) chapters on love, earnestness, and authority from Houghton's *The Victorian Frame of Mind*, Welsh's *The City of Dickens*, Miller's *Charles Dickens: The World of His Novels*, and Stoehr's *Dickens: The Dreamer's Stance*. The readings in these books introduce students to Victorian values and sexual attitudes, as well as to basic issues about Dickens' world view and style.

Because I taught this course at Antioch College before coming to Colby College, I do not give exams on *Copperfield*. At Antioch we wrote evaluations for each student instead of awarding grades and had no institutionally required exams. Moreover, the literature department agreed we did not find examinations useful in defining the level of skill our students had achieved as readers of literature. I assign two ten-page papers in this course, and my students invariably choose to write on *Jane Eyre* and *David Copperfield* and often select family- or gender-related themes.

In preparing to teach *David Copperfield*, I would recommend that instructors read the following background and critical material: the autobiographical fragment, a biography of Dickens (in particular, Edgar Johnson's *Tragedy and Triumph*), Welsh, Solomon's *Dickens and Melville in Their Time*, Hutter's "Reconstructive Autobiography: The Experience at

Warren's Blacking,"Stoehr, Westburg's *The Confessional Fictions of Charles Dickens,* and Moynahan's "The Hero's Guilt: The Case of *Great Expectations.*" My choice of background and critical reading reflects my interests in psychoanalysis, in autobiography and the ways storytelling functions for the autobiographical writer. I include as well works on Dickens' vision and on displacement of motive in *Great Expectations,* Dickens' other great fictional autobiography.

In my actual teaching of *David Copperfield,* I structure the unit according to five subgroupings or issues and spend one two-hour discussion on each.

1. Style and Vision

In this discussion, I attempt to place *David Copperfield* in the context of Dickens' imaginative world so students will see the novel as part of a body of work with certain coherent concerns and attitudes. I bring in a set of handouts and also direct students' attention to the novel's title, the illustrations by "Phiz," and the 1867 preface. We read the first two paragraphs from book 2, chapter 3 ("The Night Shadows") of *A Tale of Two Cities,* and I ask the students to comment on the narrator's rhetoric. They notice repetition as a principle of ordering; I define their examples as anaphora, metonymy, accumulation of detail both unnecessary and significant. We discuss the vision this implies: a cluttered scene and crowded city, abundance and multiplication, the urge to totalize, yet arrangement only by contiguity. They also notice that all elements of the scene are interdependent; that everything in the dark city is connected and yet ultimately alone; that the great secret, death, is inexorable and is a metaphor for subjectivity, for the final aloneness. We then look at the introduction to the appendix of *The Old Curiosity Shop* (*Master Humphrey's Clock*) and discuss figurative language. They notice certain tropes that I define as animism, dehumanization, and synecdoche; we discuss the vision this implies: living things lose their energy to the environment; objects become more alive than people; things and people become fragmented; the self becomes discontinuous; and intimacy is tempered by distance, deafness, and failure to communicate openly. The students see that animism is a figure for and principle of the aloneness they see everywhere in the two passages. Finally, I pull examples of tag sayings and gestures out of *Copperfield:* we look at Peggotty's popping buttons and ask what desire they figure by metonymy; we laugh about "Barkis is willin'," Micawber's "something will turn up," and Mrs. Gummidge's repeated assertions she is a "lorn lone creetur" and discuss the ways repetition creates character as caricature, as a grotesque and fantastic acting out of the infinitely repeatable but unchangeable self. This characterization, the students see, fits Dickens' vision—as expressed in the handouts I provide—of the self as alien and alienated, isolated, limited in its ability to relate intimately with others, and living in time only to approach death. In all this material about Dickens' vision and imagination, I am particularly influenced by Miller and Stoehr.

Toward the end of this discussion, I ask the students to focus on Master Humphrey's view of storytelling: it beguiles, it passes time, it covers over—even if only momentarily—the aloneness that characterizes human experience. We look at the 1867 preface to *David Copperfield* and notice that although Dickens' tone shows he shares Humphrey's assumptions about the function of storytelling, writing fiction may also console its author. The novel becomes a figurative child who causes its writer pleasure (at completion) and regrets (at "letting go"); the author loses his progeny but has a "favourite child," the novel we're beginning to read. I then ask the students to synthesize, to relate rhetoric, figurative language, and the function of storytelling in terms of the issues we have raised. They work to bring together figure, vision, and storytelling in generalizations about Dickens' themes of alienation and discontinuity.

As a final step, we look at the "single gentleman's narrative" from *The Old Curiosity Shop* (ch. 69), and I focus the students' attention on the metaphorical relation between the picture gallery and the family tree. We notice the contradictions here between linearity and "branching," the two views of temporality and generation the passage implies. We recreate the generational structure in the passage, I draw it on the blackboard, and we notice the curious "genealogy of daughters": mothers die giving birth to daughters who replace or repeat their mothers; daughters give fathers pleasure in begetting daughters; daughters function solely to redeem or undo the temporal difference inherent in the notion of generation, of son usurping father. The daughter as a figure of perfect repetition and redeemer of men initiates discussion of feminism and nineteenth-century values and of Dickens' attitudes toward the women in his life. Students then make the connection back to the beginning of *Copperfield* and to the figure of Clara, the child-woman and orphan, which sets up the second discussion.

2.   Childhood and Oedipal Thematics

We begin by discussing these thematic issues in the early sections of *Copperfield*. I ask the students to characterize the relationship between Clara and David. I juxtapose scenes in which Clara puts David to bed (ch. 2); Clara, David, and Clara Peggotty dine alone together (ch. 4); Peggotty kisses David through the keyhole and does "not quite replace" David's mother (ch. 4); David's jealousy about the new baby (ch. 8); David and Clara's parting as he leaves for school and "loses" her (ch. 8); and Clara's death, which restores the young mother (ch. 9). Students examine the emotional quality of these scenes in terms of tone, rhetoric, and David's knowledge as child and as narrator, and most students gradually accept this mother-son relationship as erotic and metaphorically incestuous. We discuss what incest signifies, how Freud and Lévi-Strauss relate it to the collapse of a culture around the family and to the kinship structures that guarantee the exchange of women by men. The discussion once more turns to feminist issues here. This material is difficult for students to accept, and I expect and respect their resistance. We then move to the father's role in the family configuration: David's status as posthumous child and his fear that his dead father will rise out of the grave (chs. 1, 2); David's jealousy when Murdstone courts Clara (ch. 2); how the Brooks of Sheffield episode foreshadows Peggotty's announcement "you have got a Pa" and defines Murdstone as the dead father risen from the grave to punish David's oedipal desire (chs. 2, 3); the ways David's new father *does* punish David with beating, banishment, and schoolwork (chs. 4, 5). Again these issues of paternal authority and how a father's prohibition and law structure the family usually generate lively debate about the modern family, its differences from the nineteenth-century family, psychoanalytic interpretation of the family as limited by nuclear-family and heterosexual biases, and feminist interpretations of these biases in both psychoanalysis and family history (as I summarize and present them). I propose then that we think about the "child-centered" family.

In this class meeting we move on to discuss Dickens' perspective on childhood. We examine the novel's full title and discuss the issues it raises about individuality; personal history and experience; sonhood and patrimony; and personal, public, and metaphorically "historical" narrative. We look at the first sentence of the novel and talk about heroism as a literary concept, about points of departure in lives (being born) and narratives (means of recording birth), about the ways narrative defines its protagonist-narrator's experience and so in a sense gives him the tools for begetting himself. We link these topics to hatred of fathers, David's running away to Aunt Betsey (an easily superseded father surrogate), and motifs of rebirth as explanations of how fiction engenders its protagonist rather than simply recollects his past. At this point, I ask the students to look at the "Retrospect" chapters, talk about how these chapters differ in pace from the rest of the narrative, and enlarge the discussion to include narrative time and structure. Finally, either at the end of this class or earlier, if a student brings it up, we look at the illustrations by Hablot K. Browne and discuss the following issues: the link between the world gone chaotic and mad in the illustrations and the figurative language we discussed in the first class; the ways the drawings represent David as innocent, alone, and manipulated by experienced others, as observer of events, and as outsider, although he is often at the center of illustrated space. I ask students to generalize from their observations and to discuss mimesis, verisimilitude, and representation; concepts of self-presentation; the caricaturing imagination. Finally, we compare these illustrations and the concepts of representation they imply to those of Thackeray's original drawings for *Vanity Fair*, which we have already examined earlier in the semester.

3.   Multiple Plots and Plotting

Here we begin to look at the ways subplots repeat and echo the material we discussed in the second class. I ask the students to talk about why Dickens includes the subplot that involves Mr. Peggotty, Ham, Emily, and Mrs. Gummidge. We look closely at the illustration of life at Yarmouth and notice how the boat at Yarmouth parodies and resembles a home. We examine the passages about this strange group's history and mark a repeated concern with dead fathers and family structure. We find, however, a difference here as well: this "family," while composed of non-immediate-family kin, is also a family of orphans whose fathers—Mr. Peggotty's brother, brother-in-law, and partner—all drowned. Students return to the discussion about fathers and see that this fragmented and fatherless family represents a loving and chosen unit that criticizes the oedipal antagonism of the nuclear family.

Quite naturally, we move on to the Micawber family, discussing Mr. Micawber's improvidence and exuberance and Mrs. Micawber's harried attempts to compensate for her husband's irrepressible irresponsibility. The students relate the episodes concerning debt to the autobiographical fragment, and I relate it to the continued struggle between Dickens and his father over money, to Dickens' guilt when his father died, and to the need that prompts him to write another and quite different fictional autobiography about sons and fathers, *Great Expectations*. Moving back to *Copperfield*, we notice another early figure for paternal authority, Mr. Creakle, and describe his caricatured punishing as part of Dickens' critique of ineffective or excessively tyrannical fathers.

The next fathers we discuss dote on their daughters. Wickfield and Agnes, Dr. Strong and Annie, are literal and figurative father-daughter units (chs. 15, 16). This discussion recalls the "genealogy of daughters" from *The Old Curiosity Shop* and expands to include the erotic ties between fathers and daughters in the novel, psychoanalytic theory about the family, and cultural situations that repeat the father-daughter model for authority, approbation, and mentorship (education, the workplace). It also leads us to daughterhood, to Dickens' version of the "little woman" and the metaphor for her redemptive role in *Copperfield*, the stained-glass window. Students then notice Dickens' portrayals of the failed "little woman": Little Em'ly and her desire for the status of ladyhood; Dora and her inability to create wifely order in her house. The first example provokes discussion of class issues in the novel, of surreptitious warnings about upward mobility, and of Steerforth's aristocratic irresponsibility: happiness seems at this point possible only for the lower classes—the folks at Yarmouth—who find their status acceptable. The second brings us to Dickens' and the Victorians' notion of "ideal marriage," to female submission and social-historical material about women's status in and out of marriage in nineteenth-century England, and ultimately to Dickens' own marriage to Kate Dickens and emotional involvement with Mary Hogarth. We end this part of class with some discussion of the expectations Dickens gives us as readers for the futures of Emily, Dora, Agnes, and Annie Strong.

The parallelism of female characters allows me to ask about Dickens' strategies for plotting, and we conclude this class with some theoretical talk about plot and subplot, analogy among plots, differences between plots, and ways of managing "loose and baggy monsters." I include some material here about Dickens' serial format in *Copperfield* and in the novels that appeared weekly in *Household Words* and *All the Year Round*; about the genesis of *Pickwick Papers*; about the ways other Victorian novelists used or rejected the monthly serial format; about the triple-decker and the circulating libraries; and about the rise of the reading public, which I also talk about at the beginning of the semester.

4. Autobiography and Writing

In this class, we examine a central fact of *Copperfield*: that David becomes a writer. I provide some background material on the bildungsroman and *Künstlerroman*, and students then notice that David finds language problematic early in the novel when Murdstone "teaches" him figures and reading and later when he learns shorthand. We also look at how storytelling sustains David when it earns him food and drink at school from the dispensing Steerforth (ch. 7); I talk about telling stories to survive in *The Arabian Nights* (Todorov 66–79) and ask students to consider how memory as a faculty aids David in his storytelling. We will recall Brontë's theory of memory and the telling of a life's story in *Jane Eyre* and compare it to David's theory of memory. I ask students to question David's memory of his childhood: do his many references to having been neglected, forced to suffer alone and to waste his talents constitute narcissism? self-pity? a revision of the past? We talk about the tone of the autobiographical fragment and look closely at the novelistic scene in which David as narrator recognizes his grieving self-satisfaction when as protagonist he learns of his mother's death (ch. 9). I juxtapose to this passage the scenes in which Aunt Betsey points out David's lack of self-reliance, firmness, and earnestness (chs. 20, 23). We look at David's narcissistic response to Aunt Betsey's financial "ruin" and his struggle to acquire self-reliance and discipline through his poverty (chs. 34–36). David hopes to write his way out of narcissistic childhood unhappiness and into middle-class earnestness. We notice that he emphasizes discipline when beginning a "writing" career as a parliamentary reporter, and we relate this detail to Dickens' biography and to high Victorian values.

Next, I ask students whether the novel questions David's theory of self-discipline through writing. I ask them to consider Mr. Dick's Memorial, with its figure for autobiographical writing as failing to keep out the beheading of King Charles I—the "simile" for family desire and prohibition—and its "dissemination" on the flying kite (Tick). We also look at Dr. Strong's Dictionary, linked by the years it will take to write (1,649) with Mr. Dick's Memorial. I ask students to link the scrambled names for Dickens (Mr. Dick, King Charles, inverted initials DC for CD) with the surreptitious belief that autobiography will never make its writer self-reliant and disciplined, despite David's theory. I then ask them to connect this material with other figures for David in the novel: the lunatic he always sees at his childhood home, and Uriah Heep, who sleeps in front of David's fire and in his childhood room at the Wickfields', who is his rival for Agnes' affections, and whose humility parodies David's earnestness (chs. 17, 25, 39, 42). We conclude this part of the discussion by looking at Micawber's metaphor-filled letters, at their profligacy and their compensation for failures in life (chs. 17, 49). The subterranean and mad energy of language threatens David's version of writing as disciplining the autobiographer. As we end this class, I ask students to generalize about the conflicting versions of memory, autobiography, language, and writing in *Copperfield* and to extend those generalizations to include the different theories on these issues in *Pride and Prejudice, Jane Eyre*, and *Vanity Fair*.

5. Conclusions

In this class, we examine a central fact of *Copperfield*: that David becomes a writer. I provide some background material in the bildungsroman and *Künstlerroman*, and students then notice that David finds language problematic early in the novel when Murdstone "teaches" him figures and reading and later when he learns shorthand. We also look at how storytelling transgressions. We look at her confession of vanity and changeability and link that issue back to David's lack of discipline (ch. 22). Despite Em'ly's vanity, students have trouble seeing her punishment—emigration or banishment—as justified. We notice that the novel seems to redeem her character by showing her regret (ch. 22), and we also look at Miss Mowcher's half-conscious assertion of David's guilt in bringing Em'ly's seducer, Steerforth, to Yarmouth.

We then compare Dora's fate to Em'ly's. Students initially dislike Dora intensely for her lack of competence in housekeeping and human relations. I ask them whether they buy Dickens' and David's criticism of her: has she any good qualities? I point out that "Little Blossom" makes people happy (ch. 44), that David causes their unhappiness by trying to remake Dora in his own image (ch. 48), and that this unhappiness figuratively makes Dora ill. We examine Dora's death and recognize her belief that she must die to allow David happiness as Dickens' wished fictional ending for his own unhappy marriage (ch. 53). In comparing Dora's death and Em'ly's punishment, students see David's and Dickens' desire as dangerous. I ask students how Agnes' reward—marriage to David, the now-famous writer—relates to Dora's and Em'ly's punishments. We look at Annie Strong's example: earnestness in love, dedication to her husband-father, confession of "undisciplined heart" (ch. 45). Agnes embodies the same values of earnestness, discipline, and changelessness (chs. 39, 60). She is also a figurative sister (ch. 39). We discuss discipline and incest, and students begin to see Agnes as the figure who punishes and fulfills the novel's incestuous desires; in marrying her, David marries the "angel of death" (see Needham, Solomon and Welsh).

Discussion of women characters leads to theoretical talk about closure in nineteenth-century narrative. Marriage and death in all our novels have both been "terminal." The exception, *Vanity Fair*, clearly announced its urge to deconstruct such assumptions about marriage and comic endings. We compare nineteenth-century narrative closure with twentieth-century versions, and if I haven't done so earlier in the course, I talk about Henry James and narrative theory.

Finally, I ask students how fictional autobiography functions for its author. If writing fulfills unconscious desires, how can David use writing to learn discipline? I ask students why Steerforth lacks discipline, why he betrays a happy family and must therefore drown: he has no father (ch. 22). I juxtapose this with Micawber's metaphor of the father-as-author (ch. 52) and ask students to recapitulate David's family history. They see that the fatherless hero needs to discipline and engender himself, and that in writing his autobiographical fiction, he achieves both aims. I recall the 1867 preface, and students see that *Copperfield* achieves the same wished-for fulfillment and mastery for its author, Charles Dickens.

We usually end discussion of Dickens, as with our other authors, amazed at how narrative earns so many unconscious ends, at the multiplicity of Victorian narrative, and at Dickens' remarkable achievement.

Making Sense of *David Copperfield*

Susan R. Horton

When the love-struck young David Copperfield writes to Dora Spenlow's ancient aunts to press his suit for her hand, their reply includes the phrase "with a view to the happiness of both parties." A harmless enough expression, but it alarms David "because I had (and have all my life) observed that conventional phrases are a sort of fireworks, easily let off, and liable to take a great variety of shapes and colours not at all suggested by their original form" (ch. 41). I suppose this is an offhand remark, but it has always haunted me. *David Copperfield* is a conventional book—a bildungsroman, a story of growing up—full of conventional phrases, the most common being the wistful "If I had known then what I know now" variety. But these conventional phrases in a conventional novel do "go off" and "take a great variety of shapes and colours" in the mind of the reader.

Increasingly I have come to respect the variety of shapes and colors I and my students see in *David Copperfield* as we make sense of it and have come to preface any class discussion of it—and of any novel, poem, or play—with an honest discussion of interpretation. For me, doing so has become something of a moral obligation. To do other is to shape the novel in advance for them; foster the illusion that only the teacher has access to the "real" meaning of the work; invalidate the students' perceptions of meaning and pattern in the novel; and court cynicism about literary study in the student, who when reading criticism will inevitably encounter interpretations different from those the teacher has given and may decide as a result that the whole enterprise is arbitrary or worse. I see reader response as the most effective and honest protection against such cynicism, and, more positively, I see it as the most effective teaching tool I have.

Reader response, of course, is hardly a single method of reading; two recent anthologies of theoretical essays (Tompkins; Suleiman and Crosman) illustrate its range. But the teacher need not talk in detail about phenomenological, psychoanalytic, structural, rhetorical, or historical versions of reader-response criticism to make the method work in the classroom.

I begin teaching *David Copperfield* with the simple statement, "Readers make sense of literature," and I talk about the concepts behind each of those words. The first word: "Readers." In *Anatomy of Criticism* Northrop Frye noted with bemusement that we have no word for the collectivity of people who read a work of literature (247). Especially for the etymologically scrupulous, "audience" won't do; we don't "hear" the novel. "Readers" is the best we can do, but despite the plural form, as Walter Ong reminds us, reading is a private activity, and readers themselves remain stubbornly singular in their reading. As I tell my students, it is always an "I" who reads: a singular person whose attention, for whatever set of reasons and motives, is caught by certain details in the work, who ignores certain others, and who decides what the work means in a way that most matters. This is hardly reason for mourning the absence of a singular, "real" meaning of the novel. Rather, it is cause for celebration as we watch, together, how the richness of the work and the meaning-making capacity of the mind combine to produce meaning.

What the "I" does, of course, is make sense of the work, and this "making sense" is the second concept the teacher of *David Copperfield* will address. Here one risks sinking into the mire of different theories: Do readers make sense of a novel by selecting details that allow them to integrate it according to their own psychological "identity theme" (Holland, "UNITY")? Or do they make sense of a work by using the terms and interpretive strategies of the interpretive community to which they belong (Fish, "Interpreting")? Here, paradoxically, I think the best method for making sense that the teacher can teach students is the one Stanley Fish describes as "not a method at all." I see his version of reader-response criticism as a combination of the rhetorical or structural (it emphasizes the techniques of a narrator and attends to grammar, to the linguistic unfolding of sentences in the work) and the phenomenological (it keeps emphasizing the experience of reading, or the "realization"—what Roman Ingarden calls the "konkretisa-tion" of the work). I like Fish's description of the method best: it is "not a method at all, but a language-sensitizing device, which requires that the reader ask 'What does that X do?' with more and more awareness of the probable (and hidden) complexity of the answer" ("Literature" 425).

I ask, then, that my students reading *David Copperfield* watch the novel unfold in time, note how Dickens forms his sentences, test their own expectations of how each sentence will unfold, and observe what happens in them as the actual unfolding happens. I ask them to be alert to David's language, what he pays attention to and what he ignores, whether he attends in the same way and to the same things throughout the novel. I have students consider what kind of relation David as narrator seems to create with his readers and how his commentary does or does not seem adequately to comment on and describe the action. Finally, I ask them to look closely at the language of the novel and to keep asking the central question: What does that language, that sentence form, that narrator's commentary, that sequence of sentences, events, and commentary—or lack of it—*do*?

This method has a great many advantages: It does not require great numbers of literary terms; in fact, it tends to make students aware of the inadequacy of certain traditional questions (like "What is the narrative point of view in this novel?"), because the actual narrative point of view and the responses it inspires are always more complex than that question suggests. It teaches students some grammar in a context that matters (since students cannot talk, for instance, about what passive constructions are doing to them as readers until they have the term). It succeeds better than anything else I know in making sharp, close readers of our students. It sensitizes students to how words shape worlds and our perceptions of those worlds. Even such theoretically complex questions as Holland and Fish pose (Do I make sense of a work out of my identity theme, or out of my familiarity with the conventions of literature and interpretation?) can begin to be answered as each student self-consciously makes sense of the work at hand, thereby learning something not only about interpretation but about self.

What the "I" makes sense of is the work itself, and that is the third concept I discuss before students begin to read. Some version of Wolfgang Iser's simple statement "The work is more than the text" (274) is the best place to start. The work, *David Copperfield* or any other, "stands mediately between the author's world and the reader's world and draws author and reader together in its own unique structure while it asserts its own and man's being in time" (Morris 201). My reason for choosing this particular description of the status of the literary work will become obvious to my own reader in time.

This collaborative world—created at the nexus where the writer's mind and world and the reader's mind and world meet—is the world that students watch themselves shape and that they want to describe to their own readers. This is the way I introduce my students to *David Copperfield*, and at this point I invite them to begin reading the novel for themselves.

The teacher who adopts a reader-response approach to teaching *David Copperfield* forfeits the privilege of using class time to lecture about what the novel "really" means or to lead students to see what its theme "really" is. The method itself provides something else to do during the class hour: the teacher becomes a demonstration of the method at work, saying both implicitly and explicitly, "watch me do it." The only absolute requirement I see is that the teacher must go slowly, must remember always that the object is not to give students a reading of the novel but to give them a way to read the novel for themselves. A class hour spent on a paragraph is no disaster. I invite my readers to watch me do it now. Here, as in the classroom, I make no claims for my *David Copperfield*, except that it is mine, that I have created it by putting together what seems most important to me, which is, by definition, what most catches my attention as I read and shape the words Dickens has put there.

A reader begins at the beginning, of course, and what strikes this reader immediately is a remarkable use of verb tenses. I am not by any means the first to note that the novel's first chapter is titled "I Am Born." This reader wonders, why not "I Was Born," surely a more expected formulation for expressing an event that happened in the past. The question is especially pertinent since twenty-five of the novel's sixty-four chapters, early and late, are titled in the same way: "I Observe," "I Have a Change," "I Fall into

Disgrace." Immediately, as I tell my students, we are thrown onto our own resources. There is no answer, out there somewhere in literary history or criticism, that will tell us what it means. I can answer only for myself, and to me, that chapter title seems to promise a narrative about the present moment, narrated in the present tense—an expectation that, as we soon enough discover and will talk about, is immediately thwarted.

But even before we get as far as the first paragraph, "I Am Born" begins to work on this reader. I think of that verb as it is used in the Bible: "I Am Who Am"—a usage that suggests to me something quite different from an occurrence of and in the present moment. Instead, it denotes an absolutely fixed state and calls up that which abides and endures, that which is, was, and shall be through all time. But at the same time, one thinks of a third use of the verb "am": the more common one we would use in such statements as "I am angry," "I am eighteen," or "I am a plumber," which imply neither a present moment nor a state lasting for all time but some continuing state of affairs whose end one can sometimes know, sometimes not.

It is not important to settle on the one right meaning or usage of the "am" that Dickens intends. ("It is the *experience* of an utterance—all of it and not anything that could be said about it, including anything I could say—that *is* its meaning," says Stanley Fish ["Literature" 425].) The question I want to answer and want my students to answer for themselves is not "What does Dickens' use of 'am' *mean*?" but "What does Dickens' use of 'am' *do*?" As is always the case, the question cannot be answered until the reader keeps reading with, one hopes, the heightened sensitivity to language and to the potential complexity of answers that the question itself engenders. I keep reading:

> Whether I shall turn out to be the hero of my own life, or whether that station will be held by anybody else, these pages must show. To begin my life with the beginning of my life, I record that I was born (as I have been informed and believe) on a Friday, at twelve o'clock at night. It was remarked that the clock began to strike, and I began to cry, simultaneously. (ch. 1)

Every student will recognize that *David Copperfield* begins in doubt, its first word being "whether," which introduces a mystery that only the reader can resolve. I would say in fact that *David Copperfield,* always called the warmest and least mysterious of Dickens' novels, offers here the first of the many mysteries its readers must solve. They are mysteries of a different sort than those of the "Who are Oliver's parents, and why does Monks want Oliver killed" variety, but the student need not be familiar with Dickens' other novels to watch and discuss how Dickens' narrator here sets up a particular kind of relation with his reader, or, as Gerald Prince would call him, his "narratee." In fact, the sensitive and sensitized reader cannot help but notice that much later the same narrator will begin a new chapter saying "I feel as if it were not for me to record, even though this manuscript is intended for no eyes but mine" (ch. 42), a note that puts readers in the embarrassing position of eavesdroppers who for over six hundred pages have been reading over the shoulder of a narrator who presumably did not intend that they do so.

Once I get beyond the first word of the narrative I notice that the tenses have shifted. No longer in the present tense of the chapter title, we are already in the future: "I *shall*," "that station *will* be held." I cannot help but ask what happened to the present. What is the present moment of the narrative? I discover the answer soon enough, when the present tense is used in one sentence: "To begin...I record." The "now" of David Copperfield (both man and book) is the moment of writing, of shaping in the present what has happened in the past. Before the first paragraph ends, we do encounter the more usual formulation for describing past events when David says, "I was born...at twelve o'clock at night." This formulation is reassuring—if we overlook the interjected material ("as I have been informed and believe"), which introduces the notion of reportage (and therefore of unreliability). Further, to testify that "I believe" is to inject the necessity of belief and therefore the possibility of unbelief as well. The paragraph ends comfortably in the past tense ("It was remarked..."), or it would but for the different sense of "was" the reader immediately encounters; David reports two prophecies from "some sage women in the neighbourhood," one of whom announces that David "was destined to be unlucky in life" and the other, that he "was privileged to see ghosts and spirits." As anyone can see, that comfortable past tense here denotes not past events but prophecies for the future.

If, as Leo Spitzer proposed in *Linguistics and Literary History*, each part of the literary work reproduces "homologically" the shape and concerns of the whole (18–19), I think this apparently simple beginning paragraph prefigures to the sharp and responsive reader the concerns of the whole novel. Before I have progressed beyond its first few lines, I already have a growing sense of what the novel means to me. It is a novel in which past, present, and future seem not confused but *infused* with one another. This perception is only deepened, sharpened, and confirmed the more I read. In a novel in which so many chapters are titled in the present tense, for instance, I discover that the chapters entitled "A Retrospect" and "Another Retrospect" are narrated not retrospectively at all but in the present tense: "I am higher in school and no one breaks my peace" (ch. 18). "The clock ticks," "I have come to man's estate" (ch. 43). Miscellaneous references to déjà vu, and other grammatical features too numerous to detail here, further blur boundaries between past, present, and future. To me, then,

David Copperfield is a novel of retrospection and anticipation: a novel in which the present exists only as an arena where memory and prophecy fight—and perpetually triumph in their attempts—to insinuate themselves into and overwhelm the present moment, just as the "was" and the "shall" confound the "am" of the opening paragraph.

David Copperfield, of course, is a writer. It is not surprising, then, that the present in the novel exists only as the moment of writing. But unlike the passive David others have seen in this novel, a David who merely observes and records what passes by him, my David is an active, conscious, struggling shaper of his world, always making sense of it in the way that I see the reader making sense of the novel. Further, because the act of writing is an act of shaping, because what is being shaped is the past, and because in *David Copperfield*, as we shall see, memory itself is always changing shape, I see *David Copperfield*'s active hero as always trying to capture the shape of a past that in its turn is perpetually changing shape before the eyes of the shaper: Dickens', David's, or mine.

Once a reader has ventured such a hypothesis about what the novel is doing, further reading is done with special attention to those parts of the work—language, plot action, rhetoric, image—that confirm, refine, or enlarge that original impression. As the hermeneutists tell us, this continuing enlightenment is the inevitable fact of interpretation, as true for me as it is for anyone else (Palmer). Thus my shaping of *David Copperfield* continues.

After David walks and talks with Martha Endell, he later returns to the scene of their talk and

> impressed by my remembrance of [her] face, looked awfully around for it. It was not there. The snow had covered our late footprints; my new track was the only one to be seen; and even that began to die away (it snowed so fast) as I looked back over my shoulder. (ch. 40)

As David and the reader metaphorically look over their shoulders, the past—even the immediate past—recedes like footprints in new snow. Partly because this is so, we—and David—can reconstruct, reconsider, recast, or even cast out the past. In *David Copperfield* both the recasting and the casting out are evident, and it is not only David who does such casting. One ancient Spenlow aunt, a spinster, survives in the present by deciding that the suitor of her youth "would have" married her had he not been cut down in his prime (at age sixty) by drink (ch. 41). When young David becomes "the head boy" at school, he looks

> with a condescending interest in such of [the younger boys] as bring to mind the boy I was myself, when I first came there. That little

fellow seems to be no part of me; I remember him as something left behind upon the road of life—as something I have passed, rather than have actually been—and almost think of him as someone else. (ch. 18)

Is—or was—the child father to the man? Here, David decides no: he sees the child he was as "something I have passed, rather than have actually been." But that adolescent recasting of his childhood self is in its turn cast out by a more adult David later in the novel. Littimer, for instance, never fails to call up David's younger self late into adulthood, as David readily admits.

In my *David Copperfield*, then, tenses shift partly because the self they describe constantly shifts, its past being cast and recast in light of the needs and perceptions of the present, shaping moment. It is not only David who constantly casts and recasts his past self: If I were to describe the shape of the novel as a whole, it would be as an elaborate sequence of attempts to devise a conception of self and other by constantly selecting, shaping, casting and recasting not only one's own past but everyone else's as well. Steerforth's seduction of Emily necessitates David's recasting of him (ch. 7). Annie Strong's statement that there's "no disparity in marriage like unsuitability of mind and purpose" haunts David, who realizes he may have married badly, and he tries hard to shut out—cast out—what that information portends for his future: "I pondered on those words... as if they had some particular interest... that I could not divine" (ch. 45). David is busy always, shaping both his past and his future self.

But the perceptions others have of us also help determine the shape we wear, as Annie Strong attests when she cries out, "I was unhappy in the mercenary shape I was made to wear" (ch. 45). The self in *David Copperfield* is a shape-shifter; not only the needs of the moment but others' needs shape us as they, in their turn, need to see us shaped. One recalls the negative effects of Uriah Heep's participation in Wickfield's shaping of his self, laying out night after night that full wineglass beside his plate, or the positive effects of Mr. Peggotty's shaping of Emily's self, laying out for her night after night the old frock and bonnet she wore as an innocent girl. Perhaps Dora Spenlow Copperfield had to die primarily because she had been so shaped by her family as a pet and a toy that she was incapable of accommodating herself—shaping her self—to the needs of her adult self and of her husband.

Present conceptions of self, other, and the world are of course created out of memory, and in *David Copperfield* memory is also a shape-shifter. Remembering Traddles' face, David says it "impresses me more in the remembrance than it did in reality" (ch. 41), a sentiment that suggests no necessary correlation between the present import of the moment and its effect in retrospect. If *David Copperfield* explores anything systematically, it explores the nature and workings of memory: the specific ways in which it intrudes on and shapes the present. *David Copperfield*, like all of Dickens' novels, brims over with specific details: the carving on a gravestone, the curve of an ear, the whorl of breath in the cold, the carving on a desk top or a window sill. And the simplest of these details, even the "irrelevant" detail, can become a snare, so that David is liable to be ambushed by the past, unexpectedly, at any moment. As the adult David walks to Dr. Strong's, he hears the crunch and smells the odor of autumn leaves, and all of his past suddenly springs into consciousness: "I remember how the leaves smelt like our garden at Blunderstone as we trod them underfoot, and how the old, unhappy feeling seemed to go by, on the sighing wind" (ch. 45). It takes but "the scent of a geranium leaf" to call up forever in David's mind and heart his delirious courtship of Dora (ch. 26)—as, we might add, it took but a certain smell to call up the blacking warehouse to the adult Dickens. Here, finally, we can begin to see the import of the present-tense chapter titles, which announce what *was* in a tense that denotes what *is*: the past really persists in the present, like it or not. We are thrust into this insight by what Richard Hugo would have called "the triggering detail."

But even the triggering detail is a shape-shifter. After David's schooling at Dr. Strong's, the "two great aloes in tubs" outside his home become "ever since, by association...symbolical to me of silence and retirement" (ch. 16). Yet not much later in the narrative those same aloes become associated, in a more recent memory, with Dr. Strong's painful misperception that his wife doesn't love him and with David's growing awareness that he has made a poor marriage:

> I had no pleasure in thinking, any more, of the grave old broad-leaved aloe-trees which remained shut up in themselves a hundred years together.... It was as if the tranquil sanctuary of my boyhood had been sacked before my face, and its peace and honour given to the winds. (ch. 19)

Newer memories reshape older. Memories cast their tentacles into the future, changing its shape as well:

> When I measured Dora's finger for a ring that was to be made of Forget-me-nots, and when the jeweller, to whom I took the measure, found me out, and laughed over his order-book, and charged me anything he liked for the pretty little toy, with its blue stones—so associated in my remembrance with Dora's hand, that yesterday, when I saw such another, by chance, on the finger of my own

daughter, there was a momentary stirring in my heart, like pain! (ch. 33)

The biographical critic will of course hear echoes of Dickens' feelings for his sister-in-law Mary Hogarth and think of the ring he bought for her. But in the pattern I describe, the mingling of past, present, and future matters most. The aloe David passes today is a shape-shifter: it simply is not the same aloe he had passed as a child. In this way present and future change the past, just as the past changes present and future, and thus we can come to see the relevance of Dickens' chapter title, which recalls the biblical "I Am Who Am." The abiding and enduring present that contains both past and future is what *David Copperfield* is about.

As this pattern shapes itself in my mind, it grows, taking in increasingly and systematically all the details of the novel. The shape-shifting quality of self, memory, and perception is reproduced at the peripheries of David's world throughout the novel, but especially in the childhood chapters, where people shift from human to beast and back again and lurch out to grab the unsuspecting child just as memory lurches out to grab us at unsuspecting moments. Recall, for example, the old pawnbroker with claws for hands, who squawks "O Goroo! Goroo!" at David; the trampers, "most ferocious looking ruffians, who stared at me as I went by: and stopped, perhaps, and called after me to come back and speak to them, and when I took to my heels, stoned me" (ch. 13); and the Heeps, mother and son, who hover over the Wickfield home "like two bats hanging over the whole house and darkening it with their ugly forms" (ch. 39). Uriah changes his shape again and again, becoming a page later "a malevolent baboon," as he had been a "snake" and an "eel" at other moments.

Although the details and people one encounters are shape-shifters, David as a writer still must attend to the smallest thing around him. But despite such alert attention, he is often caught unawares by the future when it hits him; in fact, his close attending leaves him—and us—unprepared for it. He misses the import of Steerforth's admission that he wished he "had had a judicious father" and of Emily's "Oh Ham, I am not so good a girl as I ought to be!" (ch. 22). For all the attention paid to the landscape and the people of Yarmouth during his and Steerforth's visit there, David—and the reader—is caught by surprise when the two lovers slip away: we have presumably been distracted by all that we have been attending to.

In conventional terms, *David Copperfield* is the least mysterious of Dickens' novels. Its mysteries (Who is the strange man who so distresses Betsey Trotwood? Is there really anything going on between Annie Strong and Jack Maldon? Will Emily be found? Will Heep really succeed in getting control of Wickfield's business?) are minor, and they pale before the more mysterious—and less solvable—mysteries that make up my *David Copperfield*. The real mysteries David must solve are exactly those the reader, too, must solve: How does one shape a life, comprehend what was, is, and is to be, in a world perpetually shaped and reshaped by memory and anticipation?

When the adult David revisits Blunderstone churchyard, in the midst of his catalog of details and recollections of his past life there, he mostly thinks of the future, not the past: "My reflections at these times were always associated with the figure I was to make in life, and the distinguished things I was to do" (ch. 22). Here, again, the past tense denotes not what was but what is to be, and once again we come back to what was prefigured in the earliest chapter of the novel: the present moment that both past and future overwhelm. In *Friday's Footprint* Wesley Morris discusses Faulkner's style and proposes that the simple word "was"

> evokes both a feeling of system (the potentially closed or limited) and a feeling of boundless movement, transformation, and change within the very concept of infinite systematicity. Its metonymic nature is historicity in small, the shuffling and organizing of endlessly plentiful particularity (moments or events) before the ever present suggestiveness of order; one could say that history so conceived is "fallen" mythology. (22)

With this notion in mind, I return again to the opening paragraph of *David Copperfield*, where we are told that David was told "the clock began to strike, and [he] began to cry, simultaneously." Now we understand why. *David Copperfield* is the story of David's fall into time and history.

True to the method of reading I recommend, I insist that my shaping of *David Copperfield*—as the story of a hero always attempting to make a shape-shifting past, present, and future hold still long enough for comprehension in the present—is in turn shaped by my own needs and shaping habits. As such it is only one of the shapes the book can have. It grows out of my own responses to the work and ultimately, I suspect, out of my own needs to see the novel and the world as in flux and subject to my shaping powers. I tell my students that this is *my David Copperfield*. As the method requires, all I can do next is ask them to go and do likewise, paying close attention to the language of the novel and their own responses to that language.

Our sharing, later, of their own shapings of *David Copperfield* is, as I tell them, what the novel is "about," is its "meaning," and is, therefore, altogether more rich, less reductive, than any discussion of theme I might have offered them. I would say, with Stanley Fish, that the best defense of the method, the best recommendation I can give it, is that it works.

David Copperfield and Shared Reader Response

Michael Steig

Until recently I found *David Copperfield* one of the less "teachable" of those Dickens novels I frequently include in Victorian novel or Dickens courses: in contrast to *Bleak House*, it has no elaborate repertory of recurring symbols, no panoramic and multileveled critique of Victorian society, no complex plot, and few notable comic-grotesque characters. I had early established a standard line of interpretation, which tended to inhibit students' ability to develop their own readings without either echoing mine or relying excessively on published criticism. I could talk interestingly enough about the autobiographical materials, the child's point of view, and the pattern of sexual triangles in David's development. With Dora and Agnes, I rejected the didactic interpretation of the "undisciplined heart" theme offered by several critics (Needham and Miller) and declared Agnes not a "flat" but a hollow character, an abstract ideal rather than a real woman, which latter role I assigned to Dora (Steig, *Dickens* 129–30; see also John Forster 2: 109; Chesterton, *Appreciations* 132–35; Kincaid, 163–64).

If this sounds like dogmatic teaching, it probably was, despite my practice of announcing that I was giving students not the truth, but only a point of view. I now think that my problems with *David Copperfield* in the classroom stemmed from that novel's special kind of richness, a richness of ambiguity and of elements that tend to arouse uneasy responses from the reader's associations with fundamental aspects of emotional life—family, love, sex, death, sexual identity, and aggression. In recent years I have had some success in teaching children's literature through a reader-response approach, and I resolved to try this method with Dickens—and with *David Copperfield* in particular. What I call "reader-response" is a pedagogy that derives from the work of Norman Holland (*5 Readers*) and, especially, David Bleich (*Readings*) but that to be effective must be shaped by every teacher to his or her own teaching personality and abilities. This chapter reports on a teaching method in progress.

For the course in which I recently taught *David Copperfield*, I assigned as initial reading David Bleich's *Readings and Feelings*, as a convenient way of demonstrating what reader-response papers might look like (I shall have something further to say about the wisdom of requiring this text). Then, after some discussion of the theoretical problems, I assigned an introductory exercise on *Oliver Twist*, contributing a response paper of my own and duplicating all the papers so each of us could read the others' work. The open-ended topic required an explanation of what aspect—even something as specific as a single word—felt most important emotionally to the reader and a description of personal associations that would help clarify why the individual chose a particular element. At this stage in introducing the response approach, I usually find that about one half of the students

141

manage to produce papers that really describe part of their reading process as well as some concrete associations. (For this reason I do not assign grades to the first papers, as the approach is new for many students; on the general question of grading papers in the response classroom see Bleich, *Readings* 105–10.)

But the group reading and discussion of these first papers do give most students a fairly clear idea of what one can address in a response paper, and the second group of essays is almost always more substantial. For the second paper I gave the students a lengthy written explanation of the basic topic ("Discuss the relation between interpretation and response in your reading of *David Copperfield*"). I asked them to choose some aspect of the book that they felt to be in need of interpretation, to offer their own, and to connect that interpretation to their responses and the associations that might explain those responses. A number of possible areas were suggested—such as family and marriage, David's relationships to women, David as (unreliable?) narrator, and the child's view of reality—but students had freedom to choose. The discussion of these papers, duplicated and distributed, was to constitute the basis of my teaching of the novel, but I knew I would face the problem that had discouraged me from using this approach with Dickens in the past; the novel's length. While one might ask for response papers on *Charlotte's Web* or even *Jane Eyre* within a week or two, more time had to be given for reading *David Copperfield*.

I spent the intervening class time (about three weeks) in two ways: giving the students a detailed account of the autobiographical elements in the novel and discussing with them my own distributed response paper, which included a reconsideration of the personal sources of the interpretive line I had earlier taken with *David Copperfield*. Specifically, I tried to probe the sources of my reactions to David, Murdstone, Emily, Dora, and Agnes. If I had always insisted that Dora was the "real wife" and Agnes an abstraction, what did this imply about my own attitudes toward women? And if I had argued that the Oedipus complex was not symbolized in David's early experience, because Murdstone was an abnormally bad (step)father, what did this signify about my feelings toward my own father? Required by my own method to make an emotional assessment that I had previously avoided, I came to two conclusions. First, I had to admit that my championing of Dora as the truly sexual woman of the novel was self-deceptive, for I associated her with a girl who ran me a merry and frustrating chase for the better part of three years in my adolescence, and that in condemning David (and Dickens) for "murdering" Dora with a wish, I was actually repressing memories of my own violent feelings toward that coquettish girlfriend. Second, in making myself think more honestly about my relationship to my father, who I had always claimed was the opposite of a Murdstone, I had to acknowledge that Murdstone frightened me because he brought back negative traits of my father—the proud perfectionist who frequently showed strong displeasure at his son's failures to equal him in various skills. Indeed, Murdstone had always felt uncanny to me, but before writing my response paper I had not been able to explain that feeling in terms of Freud's definition of the uncanny—the unacknowledged familiarity of something from childhood that had become unfamiliar through denial or repression (Freud; Steig, "Defining"). The one figure I could not yet revise my conscious attitude toward was Agnes, whom I could not believe in as character but still saw only as Dickens' (or David's) middle-class, middle-aged fantasy, the pure, self-effacing woman who has loved one all her life.

I am not to be the hero of my own story as told here, and I offer these summaries of excerpts from my response paper only to indicate how I encouraged my students through example to be thoughtful in analyzing their responses and open and trusting in presenting personal material to a group composed largely of strangers. It would be naive to deny that my response paper had some influence on how the students wrote theirs, but insofar as I can judge, the influence was more in topic than in content of responses; and since I presented my response as just that, they were not on the whole too intimidated to describe responses contrary to mine.

As in any response classroom, a certain percentage of students resisted participation in the approach, and some of them denied that they were indeed resisting. I prefer not to assert the weight of my authority to cajole or shame such students into performing correctly, and I find that something in virtually every paper bears on the question of response and allows for questioning and discussion, for the clarification and development of what a student may only have suggested in the paper. I shall give an example later of how unstated autobiographical details may come out in classroom discussion to everyone's enlightenment, but I first want to summarize a few of the fullest and most detailed papers and their discussion, in order to suggest what the shared response method can accomplish not only in developing individual self-understanding but in creating new critical insights of a kind that, in another context, might seem "objective."

The question of Dickens' women, as might be expected from both the way I had presented my responses and the predominantly female enrollment in the course, was most frequently chosen as a topic. But some of the results were unexpected and enlightening. Many factors can influence the way students write response papers, apart from questions the instructor may raise initially. In the class I am referring to, one woman (Student A) made her paper available to us somewhat ahead of the due date, and it clearly affected some subsequent contributions. (This can in fact promote a kind of dialogue that may be more difficult to achieve when all papers come in at once.) On the face of it, this paper, by a student in her late thirties, was unsophisticated, even sentimental. It seemed to take straight what professional critics often think of as the most "Victorian" values apparent in Dickens' overt intentions. Student A had no difficulty with the marriage to Agnes as the ultimate, believable goal of David's development, and she set up a dichotomy between the "spiritual" and "sensual" sides of David's relationships to women, claiming that the pre-Murdstone "Edenic" world, with Clara Copperfield "like the Virgin Mary . . . young, innocent, and fair," is regained only in Agnes. But the paper's dominant theme seemed to be family problems, with David's unhappy childhood, the financial difficulties of the Micawbers, Emily's desertion of the Peggottys, and Mr. Wickfield's alcoholic mourning serving as examples. For this student the two themes intersect in David's marriage to Dora: "By reacting to his sensual impulses rather than his spiritual ones, David becomes entrapped in an unsuitable marriage. Agnes, on the other hand, offers a more meaningful bond. She radiates an enduring quality in her love."

Without the personal associations subsequently described by A in her paper, it would have been difficult or impossible to tell how much of this interpretation involved stock responses and how much was an exploration of the genuine experience of reading. She too had an absent father in early childhood and then a stepfather by whom she felt rejected—"Like David I felt there was one appetite too many at the table." Her education was also interrupted after high school, her early married life full of financial difficulties as well as conflicts with relatives. It appears, therefore, that her unquestioning acceptance of David's marriage to Agnes had much to do with the development of her own life toward a present feeling of fulfillment and stability as a wife, mother, and successful university student. In reading David's life story, this student found so many striking parallels to her own that other questions became relatively unimportant.

The main difficulty members of the class had with A's paper was her distinction between the sensual and the spiritual, but in discussion it became apparent that this dichotomy resulted from a somewhat unreflective use of terms, which had trapped her into seeming to deny the presence of sensuality in successful marriages. Indeed, A was visibly embarrassed when this was pointed out and took pains to clarify her intention. Interestingly, she was the student who, at the beginning of the course, had expressed the greatest doubt and anxiety about the response approach, specifically because it would prevent her from relying on published criticism to frame her arguments; yet she was the most productive writer in the class, able to relate interpretation to response and to explain response on the basis of detailed associations.

This student's way of combining a literal or even "Victorian" reading with genuine self-reflection seemed to me to implicate teachers of literature, and perhaps of Dickens in particular, in a situation rarely acknowledged (as far as I know) in Anglo-American criticism or theory but given considerable attention in West Germany. Dieter Richter has called it "*the contradiction between institutional reading and private reading*," referring to the problem of students reading "differently than teachers wish"—that is, not reading critically but instead participating in "sympathetic, vicarious identification with texts" or, more likely, developing "something on the order of a double reading morality: in the reading institutions they behave like critical readers, once outside of them they behave quite differently" (31, 36; italics in original). Richter blames this problem on the tendency of teachers to encourage students to treat the literary work as a distanced object instead of taking into account the kind of elective reading students choose and using the individual experiences of private reading as a starting point from which to explore social and cultural values. (Richter is talking about what he considers the failure of such teachers in their attempt to promote a "progressive" kind of critical reading, informed by socialist values.) My own use of these concepts is in an embryonic stage, but they suggest a new direction for the response classroom, beyond the "identity theme" of Norman Holland (*5 Readers*), the exploration of "interpretive strategies" by Stanley Fish (*Is There a Text?*), or the "negotiation" of response into knowledge of David Bleich (*Subjective Criticism*).

Another example of a seemingly "private" reading came out when I again raised the question I had posed in my own paper, of Agnes Wickfield's credibility as a character. Surprisingly, student B, whom I had thought the most self-consciously feminist student in the class, strongly insisted on the reality of Agnes. At first she could give no explanation, but when we had her paper in hand the basis of this response became clear: student B identified strongly with Agnes, not because of the religious aura with which David surrounds her but rather because B saw Agnes' lack of assertiveness in her love for David as a quality of her own in adolescence. Neither pretty nor popular in high school, B had always been the one to whom boys came for "understanding," usually of their problems with other girls. She acknowledged that to some extent her acting as consoler was a conscious strategy to attract boys but remarked wryly that it never worked—they always went off with the girls who could play successfully the baby-doll role, which she connected with Dora. This set of associations opened up for me, at least, a possibility I had never considered: that while Agnes was from David's point of view a confidante and guardian angel, someone whom he could not love as he had loved Emily or Dora, from Agnes' standpoint the matter might look quite different. Dickens does not give us the psychologically complex character seen by B, since he shows us Agnes only through David's eyes, but B's strong conviction, based on personal associations, that Agnes is more than an abstract ideal enabled me for the first time to imagine psychological motivations for a character whom I had previously seen as curiously missing from the novel.

In class discussion, this insight called into question David's credibility as narrator and the adequacy of his understanding of himself or another— whether the latter be Agnes or Steerforth. A third paper focused on what student C called the paradox that the female characters are more complex and interesting than the males and yet are seen only from a limited masculine viewpoint. C felt especially incensed by the treatment of Emily, who is defined by the males (David, Ham, Daniel Peggotty) solely through her function for men—her status changing, after she succumbs to Steerforth, from that of an adored child and young woman to a kind of "neuter," a woman for whom a husband (or another lover) is unthinkable. The argument that this was a standard Victorian attitude (a generalization that would not be fully accurate) would not answer the irritation of the student, who traced her own anger back to adolescence, when "peer pressure makes it clear that a girl's social, and by inference, other worth as a human is directly related to her desirability by males." This perception, response, and association led C to question David's reliability and ultimate maturity and to express a wish for Agnes to be more than what David shows us: an angel who "cannot be sexy in David's world." This student also picked up on the reference to Betsey Trotwood as "masculine," pointing out that Betsey "does not need the male counterpoint as others do, in order to be 'valid.' " But this point in turn aroused an association with her father, who wanted C, the second of three girls, to be his "boy," and although she herself did not make the connection, it seems likely that this memory aggravated her resentment of Dickens' (or David's) limited vision of women.

Student D's paper on this general topic, written partly in response to student A's paper, was the only one in the lot that saw some positive worth in Dora, on the subjective ground that childlikeness is an important trait of D herself, especially in contrast to her Germanic upbringing. She wondered whether the problem with sensuality in the novel is not that it is false but that it is, for David, dangerous. Student D had the rare ability to use Freudian concepts that demonstrated a personal understanding through her own experiences, and not just a mechanical allegorizing of the text in psychoanalytic terms. She was thus able, on the basis of considerable self-awareness, to be more open to and less critical of David's shortcomings. Indeed, this student saw something of herself not only in Dora but in Steerforth (the need to dominate) and Rosa Dartle (a tendency towards depression and self-destructiveness when she felt bereft of love). And she was more clear-sighted than I and most of the other students were about Clara Copperfield, whom she described as calculating and manipulative— something I had always sensed but never acknowledged, because I was too engrossed with my schema, which identified Clara, Emily, and Dora as the sexual women in David's life.

The aim of teaching with student papers as the main focus is to make possible a noncompetitive sharing of responses and ideas, so that the class (and the teacher) may assess several viewpoints and recognize the subjective basis of each. I find that the outcome in any given class is never predictable and that the teacher must relinquish some control, although it should be obvious that I was responsible in part for the direction some of the discussions took. One criticism that has been leveled at such theorists as Norman Holland and David Bleich is that their pedagogical approach tends to fragment response into a series of discrete, individualistic positions and leaves no way to take social and cultural factors into account. Although I did not make much of such factors myself, the material was there to be worked with further—perhaps according to Dieter Richter's suggestions. For example, the most obvious area of common concern—the awareness that women in particular are a "problem" for modern readers of Dickens' novel—had cultural and social implications. Another likely productive approach would be to consider the extent to which a continuity rather than a break with Victorian culture generates particular responses. Such continuity was obviously present in student A's paper, although I would have felt presumptuous encouraging her to become more critical, at age thirty-eight, of her values (and indeed the heterogeneousness of my university's student body, in contrast to David Bleich's students at Indiana or the groups of German students Richter refers to, presents a special difficulty—but also special challenges—in using the response approach). Certainly I could ask students to write about cultural issues, such as the continuity of Victorian values, as well as about personal matters. In British Columbia, most university students can remember being strapped or paddled in school and thus have at least one obvious connection to *David Copperfield* that many American students may not.

I cannot leave my account of this class without commenting on the five male students, who ranged in age from mid-twenties to late forties, took little part in considering the credibility and significance of the women characters in *David Copperfield*, and on the whole, provided few personal associations. One man, in fact, took the opportunity of the *David Copperfield* paper to attack Bleich on the ground that it was impossible for a bunch of strangers to share honestly the intimate details that governed their responses; another wrote a long, interesting, but confused paper trying to show that interpretation is inseparable from response. The first student attacked subjective criticism partly to evade talking about his responses, but one cue I have taken from his paper is that I would be unwise to assign *Readings and Feelings* in the future, for it is more useful to have students attack what they see as *my* theoretical position—and thus uncover the real areas of disagreement—than to have a book they can use as a scapegoat.

But one male student's paper did provoke discussion that uncovered an interesting bit of personal material. Virtually all the students who talked

about David's problems with Murdstone condemned the latter unequivo-
cally, but one man went so far in the opposite direction as to insist that
Murdstone's resentment of David was justified. His paper gave few clues to
the origin of this response, and many of us suspected that it was pure
orneriness. However, after some probing the crucial fact emerged: this
man had had a relationship with a divorced woman, but it ended because
of her young son's insurmountable hostility to his mother's lover. A certain
amount of hilarity resulted from this revelation, but I don't think any of us
dismissed the response as idiosyncratic; I know I did not, for, as with the
sudden insight into the potential psychological depth of Agnes, I now saw
Murdstone and David's relationship from the stepfather's side. And if this
class gained any objective knowledge about *David Copperfield*, it was
perhaps that the way Dickens restricts point of view to David implies other
realities, as the other characters might see them, which the reader can
construct only on an inferential and inevitably subjective basis. This insight
parallels the proposition that new knowledge, new realities, can arise from
sharing a range of responses to a literary work.

PARTICIPANTS IN SURVEY OF DICKENS INSTRUCTORS

The following scholars and teachers of Dickens generously agreed to participate in the survey of approaches to teaching *David Copperfield* that preceded preparation of this volume. Without their assistance and support, the volume would not have been possible.

Richard Adicks, University of Central Florida; Celia Anderson, Eastern Connecticut State College; Emma Argulewicz, New York State University College, New Paltz; Robert Bledsoe, University of Texas, El Paso; Peter S. Bracher, Wright State University; Gerry H. Brookes, University of Nebraska; Jerome H. Buckley, Harvard University; Jean Ferguson Carr, Carnegie-Mellon University; John Archer Carter, Wake Forest University; Ellen M. Casey, University of Scranton; Miriam Cheikin, Nassau Community College; Beverly Lyon Clark, Wheaton College; Philip Cohen, University of Iowa; Irving P. Cummings, University of Connecticut; Curtis Dahl, Wheaton College; Harold E. Dailey, Cleveland State University; Budi Darma, School of Teaching Arts and Literature, Surabaya, Indonesia; Carl Dawson, University of New Hampshire; Barbara DeMille, College of William and Mary; Daniel P. Deneau, Moorhead State University; James Diedrick, Albion College; Stevan C. Dittman, University of New Orleans; Henry J. Donaghy, Idaho State University; Sandra Donaldson, University of North Dakota; Albert A. Dunn, State University of New York, Fredonia; Cynthia A. Eby, James Madison University; Kenneth J. Ericksen, Linfield College; Ina Ferris, University of Ottawa; Michael Field, Bemidji State University; Benjamin Franklin Fisher IV, University of Mississippi; Robert F. Fleissner, Central State University; George Ford, University of Rochester; Jane Ford, Harcourt Brace Jovanovich; Stanley Friedman, Queens College; Howard W. Fulweiler, University of Missouri; Edward A. Hagan, Western Connecticut State College; John G. Hanna, University of Southern Maine; Susan J. Hanna, Mary Washington College; Anthony J. Harding, University of Saskatchewan; Robert J. Heaman, Wilkes College; Ward Hellstrom, Western Kentucky University; J. Gill Holland, Davidson College; Bert G. Hornback, University of Michigan; Susan R. Horton, University of Massachusetts, Boston; Raymona Hull, Indiana University of Pennsylvania; Joanne Hutchinson, Haverford College; Mary Jacobs, Cornell University; Thomas L. Jeffers, Marquette University; L. Eric Johnson, Dakota State College; Gerhard Joseph, Lehman College; Fred Kaplan, Queens College; James R. Kincaid, University of Colorado; B. G. Knepper, Morningside College; Willis Konick, University of Washington; Melissa Sue Kort, Santa Rosa Junior College; Marilyn J. Kurata, University of Alabama, Birmingham; William T. Lankford, Reed College; Coral Lansbury, Rutgers University; Elsie Leach, San Jose State University; Thomas M. Leitch, Yale University; George Levine, Rutgers University; Jane E. Lewin, American University; Dwight Lindley, Hamilton College; Michael Lund, Longwood College; Loralee MacPike, California State College, San Bernardino; Leonard F. Manheim, University of Hartford; Lawrence Mazzeno, United States Naval Academy; Jane McClellan, Brunswick Junior College; Edmund Miller, C. W. Post Center, Long Island University; J. Hillis Miller, Yale University; Jane Millgate, Victoria College, University of Toronto;

Harland S. Nelson, Luther College; Judie Newman, University of Newcastle-upon-Tyne; A. P. Panaghis, University of Athens; Nancy Paxton, Rutgers University; Douglas A. Pearson, University of Wisconsin, Eau Claire; Paul Porn, Wayne State University; Barry V. Qualls, Rutgers University; John R. Reed, Wayne State University; Rebecca Rodolff, Milton Keynes, England; Mary Rohrberger, Oklahoma State University; Dianne F. Sadoff, Colby College; Margaret Scanlan, Indiana University, South Bend; Robert L. Schneider, University of Illinois, Urbana; Elaine Scurry, University of Pennsylvania; L. F. Sells, Westminster College; Carol A. Senf, Georgia Institute of Technology; Daniel Sheridan, University of North Dakota; Scott H. Smith, West Georgia College; Susan Smith, State University of New York, Oneonta; Thomas R. Smith, Middlesex Community College; Jeff Sommers, Miami University; Michael Sprinker, Oregon State University; John F. Stasny, West Virginia University; Michael Steig, Simon Fraser University; E. M. Stwertka, State University of New York, Farmingdale; Barry Tharaud, Mesa College; Deborah A. Thomas, Villanova University; Stanley Tick, San Francisco State University; W. H. Tilley, School of Visual Arts, New York City; Richard Tobias, University of Pittsburgh; Robert Tracy, University of California, Berkeley; Ronald Tranquilla, Saint Vincent College; W. Craig Turner, Texas A&M University; Mark A. Weinstein, University of Nevada, Las Vegas; Martha Westwater, Mount Saint Vincent University; Genevieve Wiggins, Tennessee Wesleyan College; John W. Willoughby, Saint Francis College; George D. Worth, University of Kansas.

APPENDIX

David Copperfield in Installments

Date	Number	Chapters
May 1849	1	1–3
June 1849	2	4–6
July 1849	3	7–9
August 1849	4	10–12
September 1849	5	13–15
October 1849	6	16–18
November 1849	7	19–21
December 1849	8	22–24
January 1850	9	25–27
February 1850	10	28–31
March 1850	11	32–34
April 1850	12	35–37
May 1850	13	38–40
June 1850	14	41–43
July 1850	15	44–46
August 1850	16	47–50
September 1850	17	51–53
October 1850	18	54–57
November 1850	19–20	58–64

WORKS CITED

Editions of *David Copperfield*

Annotated Proofs of the Works of Charles Dickens from the Forster Collection in the Victoria and Albert Museum, London. Microfilm. London: Micro Methods, 1969. Film 96739, reel 3.

[Bantam edition.] New York: Bantam, 1981.

Blount, Trevor, ed. Harmondsworth: Penguin, 1966.

Burgis, Nina, ed. Oxford: Clarendon, 1981.

———, ed. Oxford: Oxford Univ. Press, 1983. [World's Classics edition]

Ford, George H., ed. New York: Houghton, 1958. [Riverside edition]

Johnson, Edgar, afterword. New York: Signet-NAL, 1962.

Manuscripts of the Works of Charles Dickens from the Forster Collection in the Victoria and Albert Museum, London. Microfilm. London: Micro Methods, 1969. Film 96738, reels 4–5.

Threapleton, Mary M., ed. New York: Airmont, 1965.

Books, Articles, and Films

Adrian, Arthur A. "*David Copperfield:* A Century of Critical and Popular Acclaim." *Modern Language Quarterly* 11 (1950): 325–31.

Altick, Richard D. *Victorian People and Ideas.* New York: Norton, 1973.

Axton, William. "'Keystone' Structure in Dickens' Serial Novels." *University of Toronto Quarterly* 37 (1967): 34–49.

Blackmur, R.P. "The Loose and Baggy Monsters of Henry James." In his *The Lion and the Honeycomb.* New York: Harcourt, 1955. 268–88.

Bleich, David. *Readings and Feelings: An Introduction to Subjective Criticism.* Urbana, Ill.: NCTE, 1975.

———. *Subjective Criticism.* Baltimore: Johns Hopkins Univ. Press, 1978.

Borroff, Marie. "Staging the Encounter." *ADE Bulletin* 72 (1982): 14–17.

Brougham, John. *David Copperfield: A Drama in Two Acts.* New York, 1855.

Buckley, Jerome H. *Season of Youth: The Bildungsroman from Dickens to Golding.* Cambridge: Harvard Univ. Press, 1974.

Burgis, Nina. Introduction. *David Copperfield.* By Charles Dickens. Oxford: Clarendon, 1981. xv–lxii.

Butt, John, and Kathleen Tillotson. *Dickens at Work.* London: Methuen, 1957.

Cantarow, Ellen. "Why Teach Literature? An Account of How I Came to Ask That Question." In *The Politics of Literature: Dissenting Essays on the Teaching of English.* Ed. Louis Kampf and Paul Lauter. New York: Pantheon, 1972. 57–100.

Carey, John. *The Violent Effigy.* London: Faber, 1973.

Cecil, David. *Victorian Novelists: Essays in Revaluation.* 1935; rpt. Chicago: Univ. of Chicago Press, 1958.

Céline, Louis-Ferdinand. *Death on the Installment Plan.* Trans. Ralph Manheim. New York: New Directions, 1971.

"Charles and Ellen." Rev. of *Dickens and the Scandalmongers,* by Edward Wagenknecht. *TLS* 27 Jan. 1966: 64.

Chesterton, G. K. *Appreciations and Criticisms of the Works of Charles Dickens.* London: Dent, 1911.

———. *Charles Dickens.* London: Methuen, 1906.

Churchill, R. C., comp. and ed. *Bibliography of Dickensian Criticism 1836–1975.* New York: Garland, 1975.

Cockshut, A. O. J. *The Imagination of Charles Dickens.* London: Collins, 1961.

Cohen, Jane R. *Charles Dickens and His Original Illustrators.* Columbus: Ohio State Univ. Press, 1980.

Collins, Philip. *Charles Dickens:* David Copperfield. London: Arnold, 1977.

———, ed. *Charles Dickens: The Public Readings.* Oxford: Clarendon, 1975.

———. "*David Copperfield:* 'A Very Complicated Interweaving of Truth and Fiction.'" *Essays and Studies 1970: Being Volume Twenty-Three of the New Series of Essays and Studies Collected for the English Association* ns 23 (1970): 71–86.

———. *Dickens: The Critical Heritage.* London: Routledge, 1971.

Coolidge, Archibald C., Jr. *Charles Dickens as Serial Novelist.* Ames: Iowa State Univ. Press, 1967.

Coveney, Peter. *The Image of Childhood; The Individual and Society: A Study of the Theme in English Literature.* Baltimore: Penguin, 1966.

Curry, George. *Copperfield '70.* New York: Ballantine, 1970.

David Copperfield. Dir. George Cukor. Prod. David O. Selznick. MGM, 1935.

David Copperfield. Dir. Delbert Mann. Omnibus–Twentieth Century Fox, 1970.

Davis, Robert Con, ed. *The Fictional Father: Lacanian Readings of the Text.* Amherst: Univ. of Massachusetts Press, 1981.

Dawson, Carl. *Victorian Noon: English Literature in 1850.* Baltimore: Johns Hopkins Univ. Press, 1979.

Dickens, Charles. *The Letters of Charles Dickens.* Ed. Walter Dexter. 3 vols. London: Nonesuch, 1937–38.

———. *The Selected Letters of Charles Dickens.* Ed. F. W. Dupee. New York: Farrar, 1960.

Rev. of *Dickens and the Scandalmongers,* by Edward Wagenknecht. *Choice* 2 (1966): 774–75.

The Dickensian, 1905– .

Dickens of London. Dir. and prod. Marc Miller. Adapt. Wolf Mankowitz. 10 parts. Masterpiece Theatre. PBS. Premiere, 28 Aug. 1977.

Dickens Studies Annual: Essays in Victorian Fiction. Vols. 1–7 (1970–78), Carbondale: Southern Illinois Univ. Press; vols. 8–9 (1980–81), New York: AMS.

Dickens Studies Newsletter, 1970–83. Changed to *Dickens Quarterly,* 1984– .

Dostoevsky, Fyodor. *The Adolescent.* Trans. Andrew MacAndrew. New York: Norton, 1971.

——. *The Brothers Karamazov.* Trans. Constance Garnett. New York: Random, 1950.

Dunn, Richard J. "*David Copperfield:* All Dickens Is There." *English Journal* 54 (1965): 789–94.

——. David Copperfield: *An Annotated Bibliography.* New York: Garland, 1981.

Eisenstein, Sergei. "Dickens, Griffith, and the Film Today." In his *Film Form: Essays in Film Theory.* Ed. and trans. Jay Leyda. New York: Harcourt, 1949. 195–255.

Fenstermaker, John J. *Charles Dickens, 1940–1975: An Analytical Subject Index to Periodical Criticism of the Novels and Christmas Books.* Boston: Hall, 1979.

Ferris, Norren. "Circumlocution in *David Copperfield.*" *Dickens Studies Newsletter* 9 (1978): 43–46.

Fielding, K. J. *Charles Dickens: A Critical Introduction.* Boston: Houghton, 1958.

Fish, Stanley E. "Interpreting the Variorum." *Critical Inquiry* 2 (1976): 465–85. Rpt. in Tompkins 164–84.

——. *Is There a Text in This Class?* Cambridge: Harvard Univ. Press, 1981.

——. "Literature in the Reader: Affective Stylistics." *New Literary History* 2.1 (1970): 123–62. Rpt. in his *Self-Consuming Artifacts.* Berkeley: Univ. of California Press, 1972. 383–427. Also rpt. in Tompkins 70–100.

Ford, George H. *Dickens and His Readers: Aspects of Novel-Criticism since 1836.* Princeton: Princeton Univ. Press, 1955.

——. "Dickens and the Voices of Time." *Nineteenth-Century Fiction* 24 (1970): 428–48.

——. Introduction. *David Copperfield.* By Charles Dickens. Ed. Ford. New York: Houghton, 1958.

——, ed. *Victorian Fiction: A Second Guide to Research.* New York: MLA, 1978.

Forster, E. M. *Aspects of the Novel.* New York: Harcourt, 1927.

Forster, John. *The Life of Charles Dickens.* Ed. A. J. Hoppe. 2 vols. London: Dent, 1966. (References in the text are to this edition unless otherwise indicated.)

——. *The Life of Charles Dickens.* Ed. J. W. T. Ley. London: Palmer, 1928.

Foucault, Michel. "The Father's 'No.'" In his *Language, Counter-Memory, Practice: Selected Essays and Interviews.* Ed. Donald F. Bouchard. Trans. Bouchard and Sherry Simon. Ithaca: Cornell Univ. Press, 1977. 68–86.

Freud, Sigmund. "The 'Uncanny.'" 1919. Trans. Alix Strachey. In *The Complete Psychological Works of Sigmund Freud.* Ed. James Strachey. 24 vols. London: Hogarth, 1953–74. 17: 219–52.

Friedman, Stanley. "Dickens' Mid-Victorian Theodicy: *David Copperfield.*" *Dickens Studies Annual* 7 (1978): 128–50.

Frye, Northrop. *Anatomy of Criticism: Four Essays.* Princeton: Princeton Univ. Press, 1957.

Ganz, Margaret. "The Vulnerable Ego: Dickens' Humor in Decline." *Dickens Studies Annual* 1 (1970): 23–40.

Garis, Robert E. *The Dickens Theatre: A Reassessment of the Novels.* Oxford: Clarendon, 1965.

Garrison, Roger. *How a Writer Works.* New York: Harper, 1981.

Gilmour, Robin. "Memory in *David Copperfield.*" *Dickensian* 71 (1975): 30–42.

Graves, Robert. *The Real* David Copperfield. London: Baker, 1933.

Grob, Shirley. "Dickens and Some Motifs of the Fairy Tale." *Texas Studies in Language and Literature* 5 (1964): 567–79.

Haight, Gordon. *George Eliot: A Biography.* Oxford: Oxford Univ. Press, 1968.

Hardwick, Michael, and Mollie Hardwick. *Dickens's England.* London: Dent, 1970.

Hardy, Barbara. "The Change of Heart in Dickens' Novels." *Victorian Studies* 5 (1961): 49–67.

Harvey, John. *Victorian Novels and Their Illustrators.* New York: New York Univ. Press, 1971.

Holland, Norman N. *5 Readers Reading.* New Haven: Yale Univ. Press, 1975.

———. "UNITY IDENTITY TEXT SELF." *PMLA* 90 (1975): 813–22.

Hornback, Bert. *"The Hero of My Life": Essays on Dickens.* Athens: Ohio Univ. Press, 1981.

Horton, Susan. *The Reader in the Dickens World.* Pittsburgh: Univ. of Pittsburgh Press, 1981.

Houghton, Walter. *The Victorian Frame of Mind.* New Haven: Yale Univ. Press, 1957.

House, Humphry. *The Dickens World.* London: Oxford Univ. Press, 1941.

Hughes, Felicity. "Narrative Complexity in *David Copperfield.*" *ELH* 41 (1974): 89–105.

Hugo, Richard. *The Triggering Town.* New York: Norton, 1979.

Hutter, Albert D. "Reconstructive Autobiography: The Experience at Warren's Blacking." *Dickens Studies Annual* 6 (1977): 1–14.

Ingarden, Roman. *The Literary Work of Art: An Investigation on the Borderlines of Ontology, Logic, and the Theory of Literature.* Trans. and introd. George G. Grabowicz. Evanston: Northwestern Univ. Press, 1973.

Iser, Wolfgang. *The Implied Reader: Patterns of Communication in Prose Fiction from Bunyan to Beckett.* Baltimore: Johns Hopkins Univ. Press, 1974.

James, Henry. Preface. *The Ambassadors.* By James. New York: Scribners, 1909. xvii–xviii.

James, Jean M. Translator's Introduction. *Rickshaw.* By Lao She. Trans. James. Honolulu: Univ. Press of Hawaii, 1979. vii–xi.

Johnson, E. D. H. *Charles Dickens: An Introduction to His Novels*. New York: Random, 1969.

Johnson, Edgar. *Charles Dickens: His Tragedy and Triumph*. New York: Simon, 1952; abridged paperback, New York: Viking, 1977.

———. "Dickens: The Dark Pilgrimage." In *Charles Dickens, 1812–1970: A Centennial Volume*. Ed. E. W. F. Tomlin. New York: Simon, 1969. 41–63.

Joyce, James. *Ulysses*. New York: Modern Library, 1961.

Katarsky, I. *Dikkens v Rossii [Dickens in Russia]*. Moscow: Nauka, 1966.

Kermode, Frank. *The Sense of an Ending: Studies in the Theory of Fiction*. New York: Oxford Univ. Press, 1967.

Kincaid, James R. *Dickens and the Rhetoric of Laughter*. Oxford: Clarendon, 1971.

Kucich, John. *Excess and Restraint in Dickens*. Athens: Univ. of Georgia Press, 1981.

Lacan, Jacques. "The Function of Language in Psychoanalysis." In his *The Language of the Self*. Ed. and trans. Anthony Wilden. Baltimore: Johns Hopkins Univ. Press, 1968. 1–87.

Lambert, Gavin. "Shadow upon Shadow upon Shadow: Hugh Walpole in Hollywood." *Sight and Sound* 23.2 (Oct.-Dec. 1953): 78–82.

Landow, George P., ed. *Approaches to Victorian Autobiography*. Athens: Ohio Univ. Press, 1979.

Lanham, Richard. *Revising Prose*. New York: Scribners, 1979.

Lankford, William. "'The Deep of Time': Narrative Order in *David Copperfield*." *ELH* 46 (1979): 452–67.

Lary, N. M. *Dostoevsky and Dickens: A Study of Literary Influence*. London: Routledge, 1973.

Leavis, F. R., and Q. D. Leavis. *Dickens the Novelist*. London: Chatto & Windus, 1970.

Levine, David S. "My Client Has Discussed Your Proposal to Fill the Drainage Ditch with His Partners: Legal Language." In *The State of the Language*. Ed. Leonard Michaels and Christopher Ricks. Berkeley: Univ. of California Press, 1980. 400–09.

Long, Richard W. "The England of Charles Dickens." *National Geographic* 145 (1974): 443–83.

Lougy, Robert. "Remembrances of Death Past and Future: A Reading of *David Copperfield*." *Dickens Studies Annual* 6 (1977): 72–101.

Lucas, John. *The Melancholy Man: A Study of Dickens's Novels*. London: Methuen, 1970.

Luhr, William. "Dickens' Narrative, Hollywood's Vignettes." In *The English Novel and the Movies*. Ed. Michael Klein and Gillian Parker. New York: Ungar, 1981. 132–42.

Lund, Michael. "Teaching Long Victorian Novels in Parts." *Victorian Newsletter* 58 (1980): 29–32.

Lybyer, J. M. David Copperfield *Notes*. Lincoln, Neb.: Cliffs Notes, 1980.

Macrorie, Ken. *Telling Writing*. Rochelle Park, N.J.: Hayden, 1976.

Marcus, Steven. *Dickens: From Pickwick to Dombey*. New York: Basic, 1965.

Mayhew, Henry. *London Labour and the London Poor*. 4 vols. London, 1861–62.

——. *Selections from London Labour and the London Poor*. Ed. John L. Bradley. London: Oxford Univ. Press, 1965.

Mill, John Stuart. *Autobiography*. Ed. John Jacob Cross. New York: Columbia Univ. Press, 1944.

Miller, J. Hillis. *Charles Dickens: The World of His Novels*. Cambridge: Harvard Univ. Press, 1958.

Minerof, Arthur. Rev. of *Dickens and the Scandalmongers*, by Edward Wagenknecht. *Library Journal* 90 (1965): 3292.

Monod, Sylvère. *Dickens the Novelist*. Norman: Univ. of Oklahoma Press, 1968.

Morris, Wesley. *Friday's Footprint: Structuralism and the Articulated Text*. Columbus: Ohio State Univ. Press, 1979.

Moynahan, Julian. "The Hero's Guilt: The Case of *Great Expectations*." *Essays in Criticism* 10 (1960): 60–79.

Mulvey, Christopher. "*David Copperfield*: The Folk-Story Structure." *Dickens Studies Annual* 5 (1976): 74–94.

Murdoch, Iris. "Against Dryness: A Polemical Sketch." *Encounter* 16 (1961): 16–20.

Needham, Gwendolyn B. "The Undisciplined Heart of David Copperfield." *Nineteenth-Century Fiction* 9 (1954): 81–107.

Nelson, Harland S. *Charles Dickens*. Twayne's English Authors Series, 314. Boston: Twayne, 1981.

Newsom, Robert. *Dickens on the Romantic Side of Familiar Things: Bleak House and the Novel Tradition*. New York: Columbia Univ. Press, 1977.

Oddie, William. "Mr. Micawber and the Redefinition of Experience." *Dickensian* 63 (1967): 100–10.

Ong, Walter J., S.J. "The Writer's Audience Is Always a Fiction." *PMLA* 90 (1975): 9–21.

Ortman, Marguerite G. *Fiction and the Screen*. Boston: Marshall Jones, 1935.

Orwell, George. "Charles Dickens." In his *Dickens, Dali and Others: Studies in Popular Culture*. New York: Reynal and Hitchcock, 1946. 1–75.

——. "Politics and the English Language." In his *A Collection of Essays*. New York: Harcourt, 1946. 156–71.

Palmer, Richard. *Hermeneutics*. Evanston: Northwestern Univ. Press, 1969.

Patten, Robert. "Autobiography into Autobiography: The Evolution of *David Copperfield*." In Landow 269–91.

——. *Dickens and His Publishers*. Oxford: Clarendon, 1978.

Pearlman, E. "Inversion in *Great Expectations*." *Dickens Studies Annual* 7 (1978): 190–202.

Prince, Gerald. "Introduction à l'étude du narrataire." *Poétique* 14 (1973): 178–96. Rpt. as "Introduction to the Study of the Narratee" in Tompkins.

Richter, Dieter. "Teachers and Readers: Reading Attitudes as a Problem in Teaching Literature." Trans. Sara Lennox. *New German Critique* 7 (1976): 21–43.

Roberson, Peter. *The London of Charles Dickens*. London: London Transport, 1970.

Romano, John. *Dickens and Reality*. New York: Columbia Univ. Press, 1978.

Said, Edward. "Reflections on Recent American 'Left' Literary Criticism." In *The Question of Textuality: Strategies of Reading in Contemporary American Criticism*. Ed. William V. Spanos. Bloomington: Indiana Univ. Press, 1982. 11–30.

Sartre, Jean-Paul. "What Is Writing?" In his *Literature and Existentialism*. Trans. Bernard Frechtman. New York: Citadel, 1962. 7–35.

Slater, Michael. *Dickens and Women*. Stanford: Stanford Univ. Press, 1983.

Solomon, Pearl Chesler. *Dickens and Melville in Their Time*. New York: Columbia Univ. Press, 1975.

Speirs, John. *Poetry towards Novel*. London: Faber, 1971.

Spengemann, William C. *The Forms of Autobiography: Episodes in the History of a Literary Genre*. New Haven: Yale Univ. Press, 1980.

Spitzer, Leo. *Linguistics and Literary History*. Princeton: Princeton Univ. Press, 1948.

Steig, Michael. "Defining the Grotesque: An Attempt at Synthesis." *Journal of Aesthetics and Art Criticism* 29 (1970): 253–260.

———. *Dickens and Phiz*. Bloomington: Indiana Univ. Press, 1978.

Stevenson, Lionel, ed. *Victorian Fiction: A Guide to Research*. Cambridge: Harvard Univ. Press, 1964.

Stoehr, Taylor. *Dickens: The Dreamer's Stance*. Ithaca: Cornell Univ. Press, 1965.

Stone, Harry, ed. *Charles Dickens' Uncollected Writings from* Household Words: *1850–1859*. 2 vols. Bloomington: Indiana Univ. Press, 1968.

———. *Dickens and the Invisible World: Fairy Tales, Fantasy, and Novel-Making*. Bloomington: Indiana Univ. Press, 1979.

Stone, Lawrence. *The Family, Sex, and Marriage in England, 1500–1800*. New York: Harper, 1977.

Stonehouse, John H. Introduction. *David Copperfield: A Reading, in Five Chapters*. By Charles Dickens. Ed. Stonehouse. 1866; rpt. London: Sotheran, 1921. v–xvi.

Sucksmith, Harvey P. *The Narrative Art of Charles Dickens*. Oxford: Clarendon, 1970.

Suleiman, Susan R., and Inge Crosman, eds. *The Reader in the Text: Essays on Audience and Interpretation*. Princeton: Princeton Univ. Press, 1980.

Taine, H. A. *History of English Literature*. London: Chatto & Windus, 1906.

Tick, Stanley. "The Memorializing of Mr. Dick." *Nineteenth-Century Fiction* 24 (1969): 142–53.

Todorov, Tzvetan. *The Poetics of Prose*. Trans. Richard Howard. Ithaca: Cornell Univ. Press, 1977.

Tompkins, Jane P., ed. *Reader-Response Criticism: From Formalism to Post-Structuralism*. Baltimore: Johns Hopkins Univ. Press, 1980.

Van Ghent, Dorothy. "The Dickens World: A View from Todgers's." *Sewanee Review* 58 (1950): 419–38.

Wagenknecht, Edward. *Dickens and the Scandalmongers: Essays in Criticism*. Norman: Univ. of Oklahoma Press, 1965.

Watt, Ian. *The Rise of the Novel*. Berkeley: Univ. of California Press, 1957.

Welsh, Alexander. *The City of Dickens*. Oxford: Clarendon, 1971.

Westburg, Barry. *The Confessional Fictions of Charles Dickens*. DeKalb: Northern Illinois Univ. Press, 1977.

Wilson, Angus. "Dickens on Children and Childhood." In *Dickens 1970*. Ed. Michael Slater. London: Chapman & Hall, 1970. 195–227.

———. *The World of Charles Dickens*. New York: Viking, 1970.

Wilson, Edmund. "Dickens: The Two Scrooges." In his *The Wound and the Bow*. Cambridge, Mass.: Houghton, 1941. 3–85.

Woolf, Virginia. "Craftsmanship" and "Professions for Women." In her *Death of the Moth and Other Essays*. New York: Harcourt, 1942. 198–207, 235–42.

———. "*David Copperfield*." In her *The Moment and Other Essays*. London: Hogarth, 1947. 75–80.

———. "Mr. Bennett and Mrs. Brown." In her *The Captain's Death Bed and Other Essays*. New York: Harcourt, 1950. 94–119.

Worth, George. *Dickensian Melodrama*. Univ. of Kansas Humanistic Studies, 50. Lawrence: Univ. of Kansas, 1978.

Yeats, William Butler. *The Autobiography*. New York: Macmillan, 1969.

Zambrano, Ana L. *Dickens and Film*. New York: Gordon, 1976.

———. "Feature Motion Pictures Adapted from Dickens: A Checklist—Part I." *Dickens Studies Newsletter* 5 (1974): 106–09.

INDEX